The **Blackburn**
Serie **College**

Theory and History
theories students encounter

What is gender and who has it? History, theory
but how exactly do they fit together? How do historians use theories about gender
to write history?

In this jargon-free introduction, Susan Kingsley Kent presents a student-friendly
guide to the origins, conceptual framework, subject-matter and methods of gender
history.

Assuming no prior knowledge, *Gender and History*:

- sets out clear definitions of theory, history and gender
- explains that gender is not solely applicable to women but to men as well
- tackles the hotly-debated topic of power and gender relations
- explores gender history from a variety of angles including anthropology, psychology and philosophy
- spans a broad chronological period, from the times of Aristotle to the present day
- includes a helpful glossary that explains key terms and concepts at a glance.

Lively and approachable, this is an essential text for anyone who wishes to learn
how to use theories of gender in their historical studies.

Susan Kingsley Kent is Professor and Chair of the Department of History at the
University of Colorado, USA. Her previous publications include *Sex and Suffrage in
Britain, 1860–1914* and *Aftershocks: Politics and Trauma in Britain, 1918–1931*.

Theory And History
Series Editor: Donald MacRaild

Published

Theory and History
Series Standing Order
ISBN 1–4039–8526–X hardback
ISBN 0–333–91921–1 paperback
(*outside North America only*)

You can receive future titles in this series as they are published by placing a standing order. Please contact your bookseller or, in case of difficulty, write to us at the address below with your name and address, the title of the series and the ISBN quoted above.

Customer Services Department, Macmillan Distribution Ltd, Houndmills, Basingstoke, Hampshire RG21 6XS, England

Gender and History

Susan Kingsley Kent

First published 2012 by
PALGRAVE MACMILLAN

Palgrave Macmillan in the UK is an imprint of Macmillan Publishers Limited, registered in England, company number 785998, of Houndmills, Basingstoke, Hampshire RG21 6XS.

Palgrave Macmillan in the US is a division of St Martin's Press LLC, 175 Fifth Avenue, New York, NY 10010.

Palgrave Macmillan is the global academic imprint of the above companies and has companies and representatives throughout the world.

Palgrave® and Macmillan® are registered trademarks in the United States, the United Kingdom, Europe and other countries.

ISBN 978–0–230–29223–9 hardback
ISBN 978–0–230–29224–6 paperback

This book is printed on paper suitable for recycling and made from fully managed and sustained forest sources. Logging, pulping and manufacturing processes are expected to conform to the environmental regulations of the country of origin.

A catalogue record for this book is available from the British Library.

A catalog record for this book is available from the Library of Congress.

10   9   8   7   6   5   4   3   2   1
21   20   19   18   17   16   15   14   13   12

Printed and bound in China

For Joan Scott

Contents

PART III DOING IT

Acknowledgments

As will become obvious as soon as you start to read this book, I am wholly indebted to Joan Scott for her path-breaking work on gender. Whether you accept the theories she puts forward or not, there can be no question about the impact her writing has had on virtually all historians. Our entire enterprise has been immeasurably enriched by her insights and contributions.

Phil Deloria, Marc Matera, and Misty Bastian have been incredibly generous in allowing me to use passages that we formulated together in collaborations that will be published elsewhere. Misty, Marc, and I co-wrote *The Women's War of 1929: Gender and Violence in Colonial Nigeria* (to be published by Palgrave Macmillan in the upcoming year), some sections of which appear in the conclusion to this book. Phil and I have been working on a how-to-do cultural studies primer. Much of the discussion of the theories of Foucault, Althusser, and Gramsci that appear in chapters 3 and 4 of this book rely on Phil's ultra-clear formulations of that material. I am deeply grateful to all three of these friends and colleagues for their willingness to let me exploit their erudition and wonderful turns of phrase, without which this book would have been a far more pedestrian effort.

The publishers and I wish to thank Princeton University Press for permission to reproduce copyright material drawn from several chapters of two books: Susan Kingsley Kent, *Sex and Suffrage in Britain, 1860–1914* (1987) and Susan Kingsley Kent, *Making Peace: The Reconstruction of Gender in Interwar Britain* (1993). I also wish to thank Palgrave Macmillan for permission to use material drawn from the conclusion of Marc Matera, Misty L. Bastian, and Susan Kingsley Kent, *The Women's War of 1929: Gender and Violence in Colonial Nigeria* (forthcoming, 2011 or 2012). Every effort has been made to trace the copyright holders but if any have been inadvertently overlooked, the publishers will be pleased to make the necessary arrangement at the first opportunity.

The staff of and external readers for Palgrave Macmillan have provided expert assistance throughout the entire process of producing this book. Don MacRaild, Sonya Barker, Jenni Burnell, and Felicity Noble guided me sure-footedly along the deceptively uneven terrain that a book like this has to traverse. My copyeditor,

Juanita Bullough, smoothed the way with speed and care. The anonymous reviewers gave extraordinarily helpful advice about what worked and what didn't, what should stay and what should go; their criticisms and suggestions made this a far better book. (One reviewer objected to my often over-the-top casual prose as 'literary high-fiving,' a spot-on expression I will remember for a long time to come.) I thank wholeheartedly all of the people involved in the preparation of this book.

As always, my love and appreciation go to Anne Davidson, who brought me tea, jokes, and encouragement at just the right moments.

Introduction: Gender: What Is It? Who Has It?

If you are reading this book, chances are you are enrolled in a course that hopes to teach you at least one – and probably more – of three things: how historians think about and write history; how historians use theory to write history; and how historians use theories about gender to write history. For a long time, especially in the English-speaking world, history and theory were thought to be enterprises that should have nothing to do with one another, but fortunately, over the past few decades, even the most adamant among us have come to recognize that pretending history can be theory-free itself rests upon a theory. (In fact, this series contains a book called *Empiricism and History*, by Stephen Davies. You should read it.)

History, theory, gender. We'll take them in turn.

Historians study the past: we study change over time and we produce scholarship about it. This may seem entirely straightforward to you, but when we look more closely, this process gets far more complicated. For one thing, there is no 'past' out there just waiting for us to faithfully reproduce it, even if we had all the time and all the resources in the world to try to do so. Our articles, books, and lectures *interpret* the past, they *reconstruct* the past on the basis of the questions we have decided to ask of it. For another, what we decide to study, how we decide to study it, and the questions we raise to do so are all influenced by the time and place in which we live. What questions do we think are most important? About whom and what do we ask those questions? What people and which events deserve our attention? Who and what do we leave out? – for we always have to leave out someone or something. The answers to these queries determine what our histories look like, and because the queries and the answers they yield themselves change over time, history itself has a history. The history I lay out in the chapters that follow, for instance, is focused almost exclusively on Anglophone countries, a product both of my location in the United States and my training as a British historian in American universities. (You could walk away after reading this book with the impression that no one but English-speaking people ever wrote about gender, an impression that would be wildly misplaced.) My background and my situatedness in a particular academic context – and, indeed, the material limitations of a book of this size, addressed to a particular audience at a particular pricing point – incline me toward certain approaches to the subjects I have chosen to put forward. I've left out a great deal, and not everyone will agree with my choices or my frames of reference.

But, you might ask, what is the value of reading or writing history if all it is is an exercise in subjective self-indulgence? If that were all it is, then you're right, there would be no value. But the discipline of history does have rules, as the term 'discipline' suggests: it implies a kind of regulation or ordering of knowledge that must be adhered to if one is allowed to claim membership in it. Not just anybody, in other words, can declare herself a 'historian.' The member of the discipline has to have followed a rigorous course of study determined by an exclusive group of professional practitioners of the discipline; to have passed an examination certifying her as possessed of the knowledge required by the discipline; and to have produced her own small subset of knowledge defined as part of the discipline and following the rules laid out by its professional practitioners. In the Anglophone world today, this sequence produces a Ph.D. dissertation, which then allows one to teach at university or college level. The rules of the discipline, policed by professional associations, journals, publishers, hiring committees, and departmental tenure, and promotion committees, determine what kinds of subjects we study and write about, what kinds of evidence we use, how we use that evidence, and what kinds of 'truths' we aspire to prove. The best historical work hews closely to evidence: we strive to persuade readers of our arguments on the basis of the evidence we mobilize to support them.

What about theory? We might think about it as an engagement with *ideas* that arise out of evidence and that help to explain the broader meanings and the human significance that attaches to our interpretive work. The skilled interpreter of historical texts or events is always informed by theories and contexts, and constantly moves between them. Theory is difficult. It often uses abstruse language, and while it builds upon interpretations, it also builds upon *other* theory, as you will see in the chapters that follow. These discussions can get tedious, but we all have to engage theory and its difficult concepts. I've tried to eliminate as much jargon as I can, but sometimes it's just not possible.

Finally, what is this thing called 'gender'? We conventionally think of it as the cultural or social qualities attached to a sexed body. Questions about gender have plagued thinkers for millennia and have yielded answers that range from the ridiculous to the truly crazy. To this day, ideas about gender – about the differences between male and female, men and women, masculine and feminine – inform how we think about almost everything that crosses our paths in the course of our everyday lives. In areas ranging from politics to pub life, music to the military, video games to variations on a theme, babies to beer, automobiles to astrophysics, fashion to football – what our society assumes about differences between male and female and beliefs about the ways men and women and boys and girls do or are supposed to act bombard our senses. We use ideas about femininity and masculinity to sell every product under the sun; to press for conservative or liberal policies; to justify aggression or plead for peace – and we usually don't even know we are doing it. Gender is both everywhere and nowhere at the same time.

Everywhere because notions about sexual difference seem the most readily available examples to explain or justify a variety of situations. We're so familiar with what we regard as differences between men and women that we turn almost automatically to gender as a metaphor for other relationships. And *nowhere* because we believe, mostly, that those differences are natural, that they derive from nature. We don't notice when we use them to sell, argue, justify, or challenge. But it turns out that what philosophers, religious thinkers, scientists, physicians, psychiatrists, sociologists, anthropologists, historians, politicians, and educators have been telling us about gender over the past 2000 years has changed frequently. That is to say, these ideas have a *history*, they change over time and vary by geographic or cultural context. They aren't natural. We make them up – we *construct* them, as we say today, and as a society we usually do so in order to further a particular political, cultural, economic, or social agenda.

This last bit about using gender to further our agendas raises another important point. As we will see in the rest of the book, gender is almost always embedded in some kind of power relationship. Just as gender is not natural, it's also not neutral. Ideas about sexual difference don't just sit around innocently; they are used to create, justify, uphold, challenge, or resist some kind of power differential in any given society or era. Usually, but not always, masculinity – those traits or characteristics we attribute to men – is regarded as superior to femininity (the qualities we assign to women), and this superiority is used to explain why, in most of our societies until the last century, women did not enjoy the same rights and opportunities as men. Men have served as the exclusive subject of most of our political, economic, and social philosophies; where women have appeared, they have served as a rhetorical device to emphasize or underscore the rightness of men to enjoy this, that, or the other right, not to make a case for the inclusion of women in the enjoyment of rights. For that reason, when we think of gender we usually think of it as applying to women. We tend not to see men as 'gendered' creatures, but as the standard against which the inadequacies or insufficiencies of women are displayed. It's like race: we think of race as belonging to people who are non-white, people of color. But white is a color dependent upon blackness for its meaning; whiteness is a racial category no less than blackness. Similarly, men are gendered, even though we don't usually see it.

It turns out that the way we make meaning is by contrasting one thing against another. We think and understand by means of creating opposites: night/day, black/white, old/young, male/female, and the like. Obvious, you say, and you're right. We know what is feminine by contrasting it against what is masculine. But that means that men are gendered, too; that they are assigned qualities, characteristics, assets, behaviors, and traits just as women are, even though we don't usually pay attention to that because we see those qualities as natural, as 'just the way things are.' When men dress, behave, or speak in ways we think are unnatural, we call them 'feminine,' don't we? And we do it, most often, with scorn. Arnold Schwarzenegger, the body-building former governor of California, derided his political opponents as 'girly men' in his last campaign. Beer and sports advertisements in the United States portray men in skirts or with purses as a foil against the 'real men' to whom they are marketing their products. 'Man up,' their pitchman or – woman advises them.

Why does this kind of thing work to de-legitimate political opponents or to sell beer or football games? That's what we're going to try to discover in this book. In chapter 1 we'll see how masculinity and femininity have been construed – theorized – in the West since ancient times, beginning with Aristotle and taking the story up to the middle of the twentieth century. Then we'll see in chapter 2 how western feminists challenged these theories starting at the end of the eighteenth century and offered up their own in place of them. In both instances, political concerns played a vital role in the formulations of these ideas. The feminist politics of the late twentieth century gave great impetus to the development of women's history, as chapter 3 demonstrates, out of which emerged gender history in the late 1970s.

Gender history – the history of women, right? Wrong. Or at least partially wrong. The history of women does indeed hold an integral place in gender history, but it is not its exclusive focus. As we shall see in chapter 3, gender history incorporates both women and men, masculinity and femininity, and sexual difference generally; it places men and women in relation to one another. Underlying gender history is the conviction that gender is not natural or innocent; that what societies have fashioned as masculinity and femininity have changed over time; and that by taking these things seriously, we can see how these concepts have been constructed and how they have been resisted at different times and in different places. Gender has been utilized by historical actors and groups to uphold or challenge various social, economic, cultural, and political regimes, which brings up the notion of power. We'll read about theories of power offered by three modern philosophers, Michel Foucault, Louis Althusser, and Antonio Gramsci, and discuss how we can use them to write gender history in chapters 3 and 4.

Since the 1970s, as we shall see in chapter 4, historians have been involved in an often rancorous debate over what gender history should look like and how to do it. Emotions have run high. But as is not always the case in what appear to be arcane academic arguments, the intensity of our debates have yielded easily as much light as heat, and practitioners of this craft can be proud of what we have wrought. Historians of gender have applied their theories and their skills to virtually every aspect of our discipline; they have, in fact, been able to show how gender has been utilized to structure the discipline of history itself in such a way as to legitimize it as a profession. That particular development required, as Bonnie Smith has shown so eloquently, in the context of the nineteenth century, the transformation of history from an art to a science, and the elimination of women and all that could be construed as 'feminine' from the practice of writing history.[1] History became the domain of professionals, male by definition and impoverished by the restriction of its subject matter to politics, economics, warfare, formal ideas, and the elite men who produced them. Fortunately for the vitality and relevance of the profession, those restrictions no longer prevail, having fallen victim first to the radical assertion in the 1960s that regular people mattered to history, and then to a vociferous insistence that women were part of 'people.'

We start with a definition of gender offered by a scholar – Joan Scott–whose work galvanized the field. As she would be the first to acknowledge, Scott didn't originate 'gender history,' but her 1986 article, 'Gender: A Useful Category of Historical Analysis,' became the most often viewed and printed piece from the *American Historical Review* since the journal made its contents available online in 1997, and it is not too much to say that no matter whether individual historians agree with her approaches or not, their work has been wholly influenced by it.[2] (Here I must make a confession: I don't come to this most useful definition of gender without my own particular position. Joan Scott advised my dissertation in the early 1980s, and her imprint is all over my own scholarship.) As Scott defined it, gender consists of the *knowledge* that societies formulate, the understandings that various cultures *produce* about sexual difference – differences in the physical, mental, moral, and emotional complexions of men and women that are purported to come from nature and that prescribe their proper roles and activities. As I've intimated above, that knowledge varies over time and across cultures – it has a *history*. Thus, the knowledge developed by societies about the differences between men and women and male and female bodies cannot be regarded as 'true' or 'total' or 'pure,' as much we would like them to be. This knowledge gets produced and is disseminated in a variety of ways and settings: it's not just a matter of ideas about sexual difference (though, as we shall see, there is no dearth of those), but includes things like schools and the educational theories that inform them; economic and political institutions and the philosophies on which they are based; churches, temples, and mosques and the religious traditions that undergird them; and the regular, everyday practices we encounter as we go about our daily lives, like the (now lost, maybe) custom of opening doors for women. All of this knowledge orders and organizes our societies.

Finally, and this is important, all of us use gender, or the knowledge we create about sexual difference, in the relationships of power in which we are engaged. Gender, in fact, serves one of the most fundamental and vivid ways through which relations of power can be articulated and mobilized in any given society at any particular time. It even acts to represent relationships of power that seem entirely unrelated to men and women, such as those between monarchy and parliament, or between middle-ranked people and plebeians or aristocrats, or between metropoles and 'their' colonies. Utilizing images of masculinity and femininity in this way very often affects how men and women perceive themselves and are perceived by their societies, and influences the social relations they have with one another. The last chapter of this book offers an example of how one might go about actually writing gender history. It focuses on the nature of British feminism as it emerged from the experiences of World War I, drawing upon the work of many of the theorists covered in earlier chapters. This chapter and the material in the conclusion about the Women's War of 1929 derive from my own work and that of my co-authors; rather than provide synopses of the work of other historians, to whom I could not do justice, I thought it better to provide a set of coherent treatments that I know best to illustrate how one might go about writing gender history.

So, on to some of that knowledge about sexual difference. . . .

Part I

Theorizing Gender

1 Woman: From the Imperfect Male to the Incommensurate Female

Almost every society we know of has organized itself according to gender, assigning certain responsibilities, obligations, and privileges to some people – and forbidding them to others – on the basis of the different attributes those people were purported to possess as gendered individuals. In the modern period, differences between the natures and capabilities of men and women came to be explained by their differing sexual and reproductive systems. But in ancient times, philosophers and physicians like Aristotle and Galen, while believing strongly in the differences between men and women, did not explain those differences by referring to the differences of male and female bodies. In fact, they and other ancient Greeks and Romans regarded men's and women's bodies as remarkably similar. Where those bodies differed from one another, it was a matter of degree, not kind. That is, they regarded women's bodies as less perfect versions of men's bodies, as variations along a hierarchical ordering. It wasn't until the end of the eighteenth century that scientists and philosophers began to speak about male and female anatomy as being distinctly different from one another.

▶ Ancient, medieval, and early modern theories of gender: the one-sex model

The theories about sexual difference conjured by ancient philosophers and physicians reflected the conditions of the world in which they lived. In China, Rome, and Greece, for example, law and politics depended upon a model of familial, and thus gender and sexual, relations for their conceptualization. Kinship served as the model not only for most forms of social organization but for most forms of political ordering as well. This may seem commonsensical, almost natural, but it is vital to remember that family, gender, and sexual arrangements are always fashioned within particular political, social, economic, and cultural circumstances. In consequence, they have differing effects for individuals according to gender; any legal and political worldview that depends upon a certain familial model will replicate those differing effects for individuals according to gender. Thus, a social order based on patriarchy, in which the law of the father over his wife and children prevails, underpins a political ordering in which authority rests with men, producing laws and relations of authority in which women and underage males suffer legal, economic, and social disabilities. Patriarchy has an ancient pedigree, arising at about the same time that ownership of property by individual households became predominant in the societies of the Near and Middle East around 3000 BCE and later in India, Asia, Mesoamerica, and the Mediterranean. The heads of households, or patriarchs (the word deriving from the Latin for father, *pater*), in the earliest societies for which we have written records may have sought to maintain their control over property by controlling the actions of the members of their households, especially the women, ensuring that their legitimate offspring, and not some spurious claimant, inherited their wealth. The earliest forms of political units derived from family and kin groups in which fatherhood actually and/or figuratively served as the model for the exercise of power in larger clan, tribal, village, or state structures. The making of law and the exercise of power have thus always been gendered, and as far as the historical record can tell us, patriarchal in nature, though the actual playing-out of day-to-day political operations might vary considerably.

In China, for instance, the teachings of the philosopher Confucius, compiled by his followers into a collection entitled *The Analects of Confucius* in the centuries following his death in 479 BCE, offered a guide to proper living that reflected the chaotic period in which he lived. Perhaps the single most important precept concerned the obligation of an inferior person to obey and honor his or her superior. This dictate started first within in the family, where under the concept of filial piety sons owed their father absolute loyalty and obedience. As the head of the household, his rule was sacrosanct. Similarly, heads of households in any given locality were expected to swear allegiance to their superior, the local ruler, who in turn swore fealty to his superior, and so on up the line to the emperor, who himself had the responsibility of upholding the mandate of heaven. The principle of filial piety, whether at the familial or imperial level, rested upon the notion that government should be conducted by 'superior men'; that is, one owed allegiance and obedience to a superior not because that person came from a particular family or was the richest or the strongest one around, but because he had achieved a level of moral character through study that entitled him to that respect. 'Superior men' could command virtuous behavior from their subjects on the basis of their intelligence and their benevolence, their righteousness. As the *Analects* had Confucius say, 'If the people be led by laws, and uniformity sought to be given them by punishments, they will try to avoid the punishment, but have no sense of shame.

If they be led by virtue, and uniformity sought to be given them by the rules of propriety, they will have the sense of the shame, and moreover will become good.'[1] Subjects demonstrated their respect, loyalty, and obedience through elaborate and detailed rituals and ceremonies.

Confucian thought emerged out of philosophies long pre-dating it, ways of thinking that go back at least to 1000 BCE. In the *Book of Changes* and the *Book of Documents*, for example, the binary system of opposites or polarities appears in the relationships the text draws between heaven and earth, inner and outer, superior and subordinate, noble and humble, and ruler and minister. Some 300–400 years later, the notion of *yang* and *yin* began to be correlated with the polarities of heaven and earth, hot and cold, wet and dry, male and female, and other natural dualities. *Yin* and *yang* represent seemingly opposite or contrary forces that are in fact in complementary relation to one another to form an interdependent, interconnected whole. In the abstract, one is not more, higher, or better than the other, though increasingly, and especially in the minds of Confucians, *yang* and *yin* took on moral qualities associated with good and bad, more and less, higher and lower. The Confucian Dong Zhongshu, who synthesized Confucian teachings in the second century BCE and provided a legitimation of the Han dynasty on the basis of them, gave *yang* a priority over *yin*, and endowed the Han rulers with *yang* and their subjects with *yin*. Thus a hierarchy of values seen in the order of heaven and earth was soon applied to the order of humankind as well. *Yang* and *yin* themselves also began to be inscribed with qualities such as 'vigor' and 'tenderness,' 'rationality' and 'emotionality,' gendered categories that attached themselves to the hierarchy of polarities. From the correlation of polarities with *yang* and *yin* came an ideology of dominance of some forces over others on the basis of the qualities assigned to them: heaven over earth, sun over moon, ruler over ministers, men over women. Thinking about the way the world was organized, in other words, became infused with gendered categories that established different valuations for the paired opposites. Entities regarded as higher, stronger, and better – heaven, sun, ruler – were associated with maleness; those seen as lower and weaker, of less worth – earth, moon, subordinate – were associated with femaleness. Not surprisingly, the human creatures attached to maleness and femaleness – men and women – received the same kind of differential valuation.

Confucianism has been held responsible for elaborating a gender system that presented women as weak and irrational, qualities that restricted them to a narrow sphere of life within the confines of home and family and kept them from participating in or contributing to developments in politics, culture, economics, or society. Men, by contrast, possessing the attributes of strength, reason, and wisdom, were best suited by these characteristics to operate in the world of politics, scholarship, warfare, and economy. Like all gender ideologies based on opposites or polarities, this one paints an exaggerated picture of actual realities in China, but it nevertheless provided a framework within which expected norms of behavior for men and women were articulated.

Rome and Athens also drew upon familial patriarchal models to organize political life. Romans understood their society to be a family and arranged their political and legal offices according to the principles of *patria potestas*, fatherly authority, so that magistrates, always male, behaved like *paterfamilias* and ruled in consultation with a council of other *paterfamilias*; and citizens, always male, recognized themselves as unequal to one another, just as they would be within families depending upon their age or birth order and whether their father still lived. Women enjoyed no rights to citizenship and could not hold office, just as they lacked any legal authority over their children within families, even after their husbands had died. Women, Romans believed, did not possess the moral or mental capacity that would enable them to enjoy legal capacity, to look after the interests of anyone but themselves.

Women had no rights to citizenship in Athens, either, a situation explained and justified by Aristotle in terms that reverberated across the centuries right down to our own time. Aristotle's (384–322 BCE) political theory, the stories he told to legitimate the legal and political regime of his time, explicitly constructed the realm of politics as masculine. Politics, according to Aristotle, provided men – and it was only men and men of independent wealth, at that – the sole means by which they could achieve their full human potential; the polis, he insisted, was the 'higher thing,' and the place where man, 'by nature,' was 'intended to live.' The 'self-sufficiency' demonstrated by men who headed households was based on land, or *oikos*, which enabled them to subordinate their private interests to the public good, to demonstrate the virtue required to act politically.

For Aristotle and countless others across the centuries, women had no political function, for they – like men who did not enjoy independence and who were classified, in political terms, as feminine – could not, by their nature, display the self-sufficiency necessary to transcend personal concerns. Self-sufficiency meant freedom from material necessity, especially of the necessities associated with the body. Women, for the Greeks, appeared to be all body, creatures in thrall to their physical organization who could not free themselves as men could and should strive to do in order to reach the highest good, the 'good life' of politics. Politics, in other words, and the criteria of those who could participate in the polis, were explicitly cast in terms antithetical to femininity. The polis, where men could best demonstrate their self-sufficiency and their virtue, was an exclusively masculine realm.

Aristotle, then, believed that women and men had dramatically different roles to play – for men, politics was the highest realm of activity; for women, the household, where the needs of men were taken care of, was the sphere in which they best operated. These differences, he insisted, were natural. Women manifested the virtues of obedience, men those of rule, owing to the differing levels of deliberative faculty – we might call this rationality – they possessed. Not differing *kinds* of deliberative faculty, but differing *levels* of it. As Aristotle put it, 'The female is a female by virtue of a certain lack of qualities. We should regard the female nature as afflicted with a natural defectiveness.' Women's deliberative faculty was 'without authority,' Aristotle argued; it served in the household to make possible men's participation in the polis. The polis being, by nature, superior to the household, women's rationality was naturally inferior to men's.[2]

For Aristotle 'natural' gender roles did not derive from the physical body; justification for the political inequality of men and women did not stem from biology or sexual difference. Gender – being a man or a woman – in the thinking of the ancients, was not a product of biology at all, as it would become by the end of the eighteenth century; it was a product of society, conferred by the position one held in the polity. In fact, Aristotle did not regard males and females as possessing biological traits that were different in kind; instead, like their capacity for rationality, they differed in degree. He and other ancient thinkers held that women and men possessed the same genitals, with the important distinction that men's existed outside the body and women's on the inside. Reproductive organs in men and women mirrored one another and were called by the same name. Herophilus (330–280 BCE), the so-called 'father of anatomy,' referred to ovaries and testicles with the Greek word for 'twins,' *didymoi*. He believed that the Fallopian tubes in women (he didn't call them that), which he regarded as spermatic ducts, extended, like spermatic ducts in men, from the *didymoi* to the bladder. (They don't.) The Greek physician Galen (131–201 CE), used the single term *orcheis* in his descriptions of both testes and ovaries, a practice that wouldn't change for centuries. Correspondingly, ancients regarded orgasm in women to be as vital to the success of reproduction as it was in men: orgasm produced the heat in men and women that made conception possible. In this representation, which one historian calls the 'one-sex model' in which 'two genders correspond to but one sex,' the anatomy of men and women were analogous to one another, though not equal to one another in value. There consisted, in other words, a hierarchy along which the reproductive organs of men and women were arrayed.[3]

Galen saw the inversion of sexual organs in men and women as a product of heat, the element that animated all of nature. The more heat one possessed, the more perfect one was. Humans enjoyed more heat than animals; men had more than women. As he put it, 'just as mankind is the most perfect of all animals, so within mankind the man is more perfect than the woman, and the reason for his perfection is his excess of heat, for heat is Nature's primary instrument.'[4] Aristotle believed that in reproduction the female provided the *form* that would then be animated by the *soul* provided by the male. The male gave life, in other words, to inanimate material offered by the female, an almost dead, corpse-like entity that on its own could be or do nothing. The spark of life inherent in *sperma* (seed) and the lack of life present in the female form out of which *sperma* would generate life rendered the male more perfect, superior. And as in reproduction, so in the family and the state. The more perfect, superior minds of men ruled women just as the hotter, more perfect male seed determined the issue in reproduction. Proper sexual order, guarded by men whose responsibility was to 'delight and gratify' women enough to bring them to orgasm so that conception and thus reproduction could be ensured, but not to become so impassioned themselves as to lose reason, made possible a proper social and political order. As Plutarch (*c*.46–120 CE) put it, he who is 'going to harmonize State, Forum, and Friends' must also have his 'household well harmonized.'[5] The good order of sex, in this view, would establish the good order of society.

With the introduction of Christian thought espoused by Augustine (354–430 CE) it was no longer possible to see good social order as a consequence or aspect of good sex, as we might call it. Sexuality became transformed from a set of experiences derived from the heating of male and female bodies into an unfortunate – indeed sinful – quality of humans that resulted from the fall of Adam and Eve. Now good sex and good social order could not be 'harmonized'; on the contrary, good sex jeopardized good social order. Like the ancients, medieval and early modern Europeans understood the world in which they lived to be fundamentally, properly, and irrevocably hierarchical. They imagined their social order to be a 'great chain of being,' with God the Father and the angels at the top, followed by monarchs, aristocrats, and everyone else. Women held their various positions on the chain by virtue of their relationship to men as wives or daughters; as women, they were inferior and subordinate to men, as God had demonstrated in making Eve out of Adam's rib. Woman was an 'imperfect man,' insisted St. Thomas Aquinas. Moreover, Eve's transgressions had stained all women with her sin. Construed as insatiably lustful, with sexual appetites equal to or great than men's, women of medieval and early modern times were perceived to be potential agents of damnation and destruction, requiring the mastery of men to preserve their propriety and honor and the stability of the social order itself.

Interestingly, however, the one-sex model still held sway in medieval and early modern times. In terms not dissimilar to those of Aristotle and Galen, scientists and physicians posited that men were composed of hot and dry humors, while women were made up of the less perfect cold and wet humors. Women were, the medical men asserted, lesser men, the weaker vessel. Their passive role in reproduction – the womb serving merely as the receptacle and incubator for the active male seed in which all of the elements of life were contained – offered a 'physiological' justification for their social, political, and legal disabilities. But their reproductive organs remained, as in the treatises of the ancients, inverted examples of men's genitals. Guillaume Bouchet wrote in the late sixteenth century that 'the matrix of the woman is nothing but the scrotum and penis of the man inverted'; Henry

VIII's surgeon opined of the uterus, 'the likeness of it is as it were a yarde reversed or turned inward, having testicles likewise.' And as was true for the ancients, the similar anatomies of men and women led to the conclusion among scientists that orgasm for both men and women was required to ensured conception. The author of *The Secret Miracles of Nature*, the 1658 English translation of a sixteenth-century medical tract, advised readers that women experience the pleasures both of men's ejaculation and their own orgasm. 'She drawes forth the man's seed, and casts her own with it,' the treatise recounted. She thus 'takes more delight, and is more recreated by it.'[6]

▶ Modernity and the two-sex model

And then, in the late eighteenth century, things changed dramatically. Women were discovered to be, anatomically and physiologically, entirely unlike men. They were now not merely lesser men, weaker vessels – beings holding a lower place on a hierarchical scale; they were utterly different beings now, incommensurable, almost a different species entirely. Where once women and men possessed similar sexual organs – testes and ovaries sharing a single name and function – now those organs did and were called different things. Women's organs that had not earlier had a name – the vagina, for example – now were given one. Representations of skeletons and nervous systems took on 'male' and 'female' characteristics. Sexual pleasure for women no longer played a necessary role in conception as it did for men. In short, as historian Thomas Laqueur has put it, 'two sexes were invented as a new foundation for gender.'[7]

All this happened not because scientists and physicians had gained better, more accurate understandings of the human body. On the contrary, they didn't know a whole lot more than their earlier brethren and discounted much of what the ancients had known. What had changed was society itself, earth-shatteringly so in the minds of many, and it seems that the remaking of society compelled the remaking of the female body. Social contract theories thrown up by the Enlightenment; the radical politics of the American and French revolutions; the development of free-trade practices in commerce and industry; the factory system and a new division of labor; the creation of class society – all of the elements and characteristics we identify with the rise of liberalism in the eighteenth and nineteenth centuries acted to destabilize and ultimately overthrow the old order of landed elites.

In the course of all this upheaval, a new gender order had to be established too, for liberalism carried with it the promise and the threat of equality between men and women. For many, such a prospect could not be tolerated. The potential contradiction between, on the one hand, a liberal ideology that had legitimated the dismantling of aristocratic power and authority and the enfranchisement of middle-class and later working-class men, and, on the other, the denial of the claims of women to full citizenship was resolved by appeals to biological and characterological differences between the sexes. Definitions of femininity evolved whose qualities were antithetical to those that had warranted widespread male participation in the public sphere. Men possessed the capacity for reason, action, aggression, independence, and self-interest. Women inhabited a separate, private sphere, one suitable for the so-called inherent qualities of femininity: emotion, passivity, submission, dependence, and selflessness, all derived, it was claimed insistently, from women's sexual and reproductive organization. Upon the female as a biological entity, a sexed body, nineteenth-century theorists imposed a socially and culturally constructed femininity, a gender identity derived from ideas about what roles were appropriate for women. This collapsing of sex and gender – of the physiological organism with the normative social creation – made it possible for women to be construed as at once pure and purely sexual; although paradoxical, these definitions excluded women from participation in the public sphere and rendered them subordinate to men in the private sphere as well.

These arguments at one and the same time idealized women and expressed profound fear of them. On the one hand, women were aligned with morality and religion, whereas men represented corruption and materialism. Women were construed as occupying the ethical center of industrial society, invested with the guardianship of social values, whereas men functioned in a world of shady dealings, greed, and vice, values generally subversive of a civilized order. On the other hand, women were also identified with nature – wild, unruly, yet to be explored and mastered; whereas men belonged to culture – controlled, systematic, symbolic of achievement and order. Correspondingly, women were assigned an exclusively reproductive function, in contrast to men, who allegedly held a monopoly on productivity. In each case, notions of femininity, or female nature, ultimately rested upon the perceived sexual organization of women, who were construed to be either sexually comatose or helplessly nymphomaniacal. Whether belonging to one category or the other, women were so exclusively identified by their sexual functions that nineteenth-century society came to regard them as 'the Sex.' This in turn set up yet another dichotomy, which offered two possible images for women: that of revered wife and mother, or that of despised prostitute. Both roles effectively disqualified women from economic and political activity. At the same time, as middle-class feminists and working women would argue, the characterization of women as 'the Sex' created the potential for the sexual abuse of women.

The new 'science of sex' that emerged in the nineteenth century accompanied and upheld the ideology of separate spheres that claimed the public realm of politics and the economy as exclusively male and the domestic realm of home and family as the exclusive domain of women. Domesticity invested in women the responsibility of maintaining morality and purity. 'The angel in the house,' as the ideology had it, was herself pure, without sexual feeling, passionless. Until the early eighteenth century, contemporaries believed that women's lust, as personified by Eve, was insatiable, but that women could become spiritual through God's grace, and hence less carnal. During the eighteenth and nineteenth centuries, the dominant definition of women as especially sexual was reversed and transformed into the view that women were less carnal and less lustful than men. Passionlessness was, in the eighteenth century, a product of women's purported superior moral and spiritual nature, and it helped to give women a higher status in society than they had enjoyed before. It undermined the identification of women with sexual treachery, and countered the notion that women were primarily sexual creatures at a time when their social, political, and economic disabilities rendered them vulnerable to predation.

In its early manifestations, then, passionlessness seemed to offer positive rewards for women; women had a stake in its creation as an ideology and its acceptance and perpetuation by society. As physicians took up the notion of passionlessness in the mid-nineteenth century, however, they reduced it from its moral and spiritual connotations to a phenomenon involving scientific, biological principles. Their version of the passionlessness of women once again imposed an exclusively sexual characterization upon them; it placed them in a position of sexual vulnerability while at the same time justifying anew their exclusion from 'male' pursuits.

In denying middle-class women sexuality, nineteenth-century bourgeois society paradoxically heightened an awareness of women as primarily reproductive and sexual beings. One aspect of the physicians' 'science of sex' insisted upon women's utter lack of sexual feeling; the other asserted that women's bodies were saturated with sex. William Acton, in *Functions and Disorders of the Reproductive Organs*, published in 1857, declared that

> the majority of women (happily for society) are not very much troubled with sexual feeling of any kind. What men are habitually, women are only exceptionally.... There can be no doubt that sexual feeling in the female is in the majority of cases in abeyance, and that it requires positive and considerable excitement to be roused at all; and even if aroused (which in many cases it can never be) it is very moderate compared with that of the male.

Acton believed that women's 'indifference to sex was naturally ordained to prevent the male's vital energies from being overly expended at any one time.' Not all British physicians accepted Acton's dictum concerning female sexuality, but his views prevailed throughout both the medical profession and society as a whole.

In asserting the nonsexuality of women, doctors helped to encourage the establishment of prudery in social interactions among the middle classes, and encouraged the idea that ignorance of sexual matters was tantamount to innocence in sexual matters. They encouraged the development of a situation in which women had little or no knowledge of their sexual and reproductive functions. Moreover, the definition of women as pure and asexual, while men remained passionate and lustful, set up a potentially antagonistic relationship between men and women in which men were understood to be aggressive and women to be victimized by that aggression.

At the same time that the doctors announced that women had no sexual feeling, they also insisted that women were governed by their sexual and reproductive organs. One English gynecologist, Dr. Bliss, articulated in 1870 the general view of women as 'the Sex' when he referred to the 'gigantic power and influence of the ovaries over the whole animal economy of woman.' Dr. Horatio Storer, an American member of the Medico-Chirurgical and Obstetric Societies of Edinburgh, writing a year later, concurred. 'Woman was what she is [sic],' he averred, 'in health, in character, in her charms, alike of body, mind and soul because of her womb alone.' Dr. W. Tyler Smith warned in 1848 in the *London Medical Journal* that upon menopause, 'the death of the reproductive faculty is accompanied... by struggles which implicate every organ and every function of body [sic].'

So exclusively were women represented as 'the Sex' in the nineteenth century that any behavior on their part that deviated from that of wife and mother – such as making political demands or seeking an education – was denounced as 'unsexed.' For women were not simply defined by their reproductive systems; they were, as nineteenth-century physicians saw it, controlled by them as well. Henry Maudsley, an eminent British psychiatrist who influenced much American thinking, wrote in 1874 that 'the male organization is one, and the female organization another.... it will not be possible to transform a woman into a man... she will retain her special sphere of development and activity determined by the performance of those [reproductive] functions.' According to Maudsley, nature had endowed women with a finite amount of energy, and its proper use belonged to reproduction. Reproductive processes demanded all the energy a woman could muster; to spend it in another direction would inexorably undermine the very functions that gave women their only reason for being. If women foolishly attempted to undertake study, for instance, he concluded, they risked ruining forever their child-bearing capacities, thus endangering the future of the race. Maudsley sought to justify attempts to exclude women from education and the professions and to limit their role to a reproductive rather than a productive one. He asserted that women, by virtue of their reproductive functions, could not stand up to the rigors of higher education or sustained cerebral activity.

The development of the reproductive system in women was so delicate a process, according to the doctors, that the smallest complication rendered them susceptible to mental and physical disease. Maudsley advised that 'their nerve-centres being in a state of greater instability, by reason of the development of their reproductive functions, they will be more easily and the more seriously deranged.' Almost every female disease, claimed physicians, derived from some disorder of the reproductive system. Usually the 'disorder' consisted of a refusal on the part of a woman to perform her duties as wife and mother, or, conversely, a tendency on the part of the woman to exhibit an unwomanly interest in sex. It was a short distance from defining all female illness as a disorder of the reproductive system to using gynecological surgery to cure those ills. Clitoridectomy, or excision of the clitoris, was performed to cure dysuria, amenorrhea, sterility, epilepsy, masturbation, 'hysterical mania,' and various manifestations of insanity. The source of these diseases, doctors believed, was sexual arousal; the termination of sexual arousal through clitoridectomy cured the disease. Some 600 such operations were performed between 1860 and 1866, at which time they were discontinued in England and did not resume. Ovariotomies, the removal of the ovaries, may have been performed even more often, for the cure of diseases that were non-ovarian in nature.

Victorian ideology finally offered only two possible images for women. They might be either the idealized wife and mother, the angel in the house, or the debased, depraved, corrupt prostitute. The image of the respectable, passionless middle-class lady, in fact, depended upon a contrast with the other image of the 'fallen' woman. In his discussion of pure women in *Functions and Disorders of the Reproductive Organs*, for instance, Acton asserted that motherhood provided the only motivation for women's sexual activity, whereas natural desire propelled men. 'There are many females,' he claimed, 'who never feel any sexual excitement whatever.... Many of the best mothers, wives, and managers of households, know little of or are careless about sexual indulgences. Love of home, of children, and of domestic duties are the only passions they feel.' While desiring little or no sexual gratification for herself, the modest woman 'submits to her husband's embraces, but principally to gratify him; and, were it not for the desire of maternity, would far rather be relieved of his attentions.' Some women 'evinced positive loathing for any marital familiarity whatever.' In such cases, Acton stated, 'feeling has been sacrificed to duty, and the wife has endured, with all the self-martyrdom of womanhood, what was almost worse than death.' Other women, 'who, either from ignorance or utter want of sympathy ... not only evince no sexual feeling, but, on the contrary, scruple not to declare their aversion to the least manifestation of it.' Men who found themselves married to such women complained, 'and I think with reason,' Acton reported, 'that they are debarred from the privileges of marriage, and that their sexual sufferings are almost greater than they can bear in consequence of being mated to women who think and act in the above-cited instances.' He warned readers that lack of a sexual outlet 'might be ... highly detrimental to the health of the husband,' a problem 'ultimately too often ending in impotence.'

Although nineteenth-century physicians preached the desirability of restricting or controlling the expenditure of male sexual energies, they believed the male sex drive to be 'innate.' One 'expert' on prostitution regarded sexual indulgence for men as natural; 'In men, in general,' observed W.R. Greg, 'the sexual desire is inherent and spontaneous.' Acton believed that male sexual impulses could be controlled, but not entirely repressed. The equation of respectable, pure women with motherhood, and that of men with sexuality, required a construction of female sexuality that posited its dual nature. Masculinity and male sexuality rested on the twin pillars of motherhood and prostitution. For at a time when masturbation was perceived to be the agent of a whole slew of physical and mental pathologies, the only recourse for men in a society that separated maternity from sexuality was the creation of another class of women, prostitutes existing exclusively for the gratification of male sexual desires. William Lecky, in his 1869 *History of European Morals*, recognized that prostitution served as an essential sexual safety valve for Victorians. 'Herself the supreme type of vice,' he wrote of the prostitute,

> she is ultimately the most efficient guardian of virtue. But for her the unchallenged purity of countless happy homes would be polluted, and not a few who, in the pride of their untempted chastity, think of her with an indignant shudder, would have known the agony of remorse of despair. On that degraded and ignoble form are concentrated the passions that might have filled the world with shame.[8]

The contradictions of separate-sphere ideology opened up space within which women could contest their positions of powerlessness, often utilizing the very language of women's special qualities to make their case for fundamental legal, economic, educational, and political reform. In the course of the nineteenth century, feminist campaigns won a significant number of victories, bestowing on women rights to own property and earnings, to gain custody of their children, to move about freely, to divorce, to gain secondary and university education, to work, and to control their own bodies. By the late 1880s, because employment and educational opportunities for women had begun to increase markedly, spinsterhood was no longer regarded as a woman's failure, but could be embraced out of choice as a positive, beneficial experience. The *Englishwoman's Review* noted in 1889, 'whatever may be said by narrow-minded biologists, who apparently cannot regard a woman except as a female animal, we maintain that facts reveal to us the existence of a certain number of women who, in their estimation, at least, are happier and better as spinsters than wives.' The 'New Woman' novels about independent, free-thinking, intelligent women that surfaced in the 1890s pointedly attacked marriage in their pages, espousing a decidedly feminist point of view, and even began treating the formerly forbidden topic of sexuality.

Although at no time in the nineteenth century do we find any notion of women's sexuality that is independent of men's, variations in ideas about sexuality did arise. Starting in the late nineteenth century, a whole spate of writings about sex and sexuality appeared. People like Edward Carpenter, Henry Havelock Ellis, and the 'New Woman' authors arose to challenge the advocates of sexual ignorance and innocence, of passionless women. By the twentieth century, sex theorists like Ellis had begun to recognize an autonomous female sexuality, though they continued to insist that it was harder to arouse than that of the male. Moreover, it remained dependent upon male initiative. 'The female responds to the stimulation of the male at the right moment just as the tree responds to the stimulation of the warmest days in spring,' wrote Ellis, maintaining that while the boy spontaneously develops into a man, the girl 'must be kissed into a woman.'

The notion of passionless women and the interdependence of constructions of male and female sexuality rendered Victorians incapable of conceiving of female sexual activity that did not involve a male partner. Male homosexuality was acknowledged and condemned in the nineteenth century; lesbianism was not only ignored in the nineteenth century, it was actively denied, despite the fact that romantic friendships of great intensity flourished between women. Victorians tolerated and even encouraged these passionate friendships between women, confident that they could only be innocent, pure relationships that were wholly compatible with heterosexual marriage. They did not entertain the possibility that these might contain a sexual component, for the dominant beliefs defined women as without passion. Only rarely did accounts of 'sexual deviance' among women surface. They were not representative of late nineteenth-century thinking about female sexuality, but they foreshadowed society's response in the twentieth century, when, following World War I, the existence of large numbers of single women with jobs seems to have excited the popular imagination with anxieties about widespread 'perversion.'

▶ Psychoanalytic theories about gender

Freud's Oedipus and castration complexes

Although his ideas were virtually unaccepted in the Anglophone world until the 1920s, Sigmund Freud's writings about gender and sexuality would prove to be the most controversial and the most influential in modern times. His theories, among other things, offered an explanation for how men and women take on their gendered sense of themselves – their identities and the norms and values that are associated with masculinity and femininity. Earlier theorists we've been examining believed that gendered identity was something people were born with, and saw sexuality as something boys and girls took on during puberty. Freud, by contrast, argued that babies came into the world already possessed of sexual natures. Moreover, babies and toddlers in the first five years of their lives demonstrated neither masculine nor feminine psychic identities; they were, rather, 'polymorphously perverse,' in Freud's terminology. That didn't mean that they were immoral in a variety of ways. It meant that they were unformed in terms of their gender identity, and could, depending upon the outcome of the psycho-sexual development process of negotiating the oedipal and castration crises, mature into normal feminine or normal masculine identities, or, indeed, end up with neither of them. The oedipal theory draws upon the story of the Greek king Oedipus, who unknowingly killed his father and married his mother, destroying his kingdom in the process. Freud would have assumed that his readers would have been familiar with the myth and believed it would resonate with them.

Successful negotiation of the oedipal and castration crises – that is, the taking on of psychic feminine or masculine identity by adult women and men – required that the individual repress those elements of bisexuality that the child enjoyed that did not correspond to normal gender identity. In other words, normal women were those who had repressed sexual feelings for their mothers, and normal men were those who had repressed sexual feelings for their fathers. Abnormal women had not, and were sexually attracted to women and repelled by men. Abnormal men had not either, and were sexually attracted to men and repelled by women. Normative gender identity, in other words, corresponded to heterosexuality.

Boys and girls went through the oedipal and castration complexes differently, in Freud's view. Both boys and girls, as sexual beings, experienced sexual desire for their mothers and fathers (and many other objects, in fact). In this, they competed with their parents for possession of the desired object. If they were to develop into normal heterosexual men and women, they would have to repress the desire for the object like them. For boys, the route was straightforward: observing that girls lack a penis, they assume that girls have been castrated and that they, too, might be. This fear compels them to stop competing with their father for possession of their mother, their very first love object; it leads them to identify with their father (on the basis of possession of a penis) and to put off till later sexual gratification with women not their mother. For girls, the resolution involved more complexity, for, as has been the case for all the theorists we've treated, masculinity is established as the standard against which difference – femininity – is measured. Girls take on a gendered identity in the process of noticing that, like their mother, they are already castrated. This recognition instills in them feelings of disgust for their mother and a withdrawal of the sexual desire they had for her. That desire is displaced onto their father as a symbol of the satisfaction they can hope to find someday by giving birth to a male child.

Freud offered some powerfully radical theories that promised, at least to some, to undermine the biological determinism of many previous psychologists and sex-ologists. His emphasis on the bisexuality of infants and children, for example, and his often explicit assertions that gender identity was a psychic process – and an iffy one at that, given the tendency of repressed desires to resurface – meant that gender was not a fixed and unchangeable entity. Moreover, the process by which gender identity developed was a social one; that is, it took place, according to Freud, not in the realm of biology but in the realm of the family, a social institution. But that family, it turns out – the nuclear family headed by a working father and a stay-at-home mother who cared for her husband and children – was an institution that Freud and many other theorists regarded as itself normative, indeed, universal.

Moreover, psychoanalysis filtered into much of the Anglophone world through the lens of biology in the 1920s with the popularization of Freudian theory. And, more confusingly, Freud's later theories often contradicted what he had written earlier in his life. Whereas he had first posited a psychological bisexuality in males and females, and asserted that masculinity and femininity and sexuality were cultural phenomena that required explanation, he later put forward theories of sexuality and sexual difference that stemmed from biology, and these were the ones that American and British psychiatrists and sexologists adopted without the nuances that Freud himself articulated. Femininity, argued British psychoanalyst Ernest Jones, 'develops progressively from the promptings of an instinctual constitution.'[9] While undermining the belief in the passionlessness of the female – a development that had considerable appeal for many women – many of Freud's Anglophone followers thus gave credence to the belief that biological factors determined the differences between masculinity and femininity and male and female sexuality.

Freud himself formulated his ideas about the natural psychological, ethical, and mental differences between men and women produced by their fundamentally different sexual organizations. 'Anatomy is destiny,' he declared in 1924 in 'The Dissolution of the Oedipus Complex,' and though he wasn't talking about women in that particular instance, the phrase applied to much of his thinking about women. In 'Some Psychical Consequences of the Anatomical Distinction Between the Sexes,' published in 1925, he argued that the personality development of the female centered upon her discovery in early childhood that she lacked a penis; penis envy created in the female child a lifelong dissatisfaction with her identity as a woman. Her discomfiture could only be overcome through the substitution of the penis with a child. Moreover, the absence of a penis meant that the threat of castration had no impact on girls, resulting in their failure to fully develop a superego. Consequently, argued Freud, women demonstrated little sense of justice, were less capable of appreciating 'the great necessities of life,' and were more often likely to be influenced by their emotions in making judgments than men. Such proofs of inferiority, Freud concluded, cannot be overlooked, despite 'the denials of feminists, who are anxious to force us to regard the two sexes as completely equal in position and worth.'[10]

Happiness and health for women, in other words, depended upon motherhood. What *The Encyclopedia of Sexual Knowledge* (1934), under the general editorship of Norman Haire, a prominent British sex reformer, called 'the physiological need of childbirth' in women stemmed from 'the obvious fact' that 'her organism is essentially fitted for maternity.' 'The organic need of children, which is latent in every woman, is so imperious that prolonged enforced sterility drives her body to revolt, and this revolt may manifest itself in a number of disorders and growths.' This physiological need for children, argued the physicians and sexologists who contributed to the huge tome, was matched by a psychological one to fill the 'void in a woman's life.' Lacking the activities and opportunities of her husband, and 'the care of children being the occupation most suited to her temperament, she will seek an outlet for her energy in that direction. Thus, in order to preserve her physiological and psychological equilibrium, a woman, to whatever social stratum she may belong, needs children.'[11]

Those women who refused motherhood, who continued in their work or study, or who sought equality between men and women, brought down upon their heads the wrath of many psychiatrists and sexologists, who found in their presumptions a sexual pathology. 'After all is said and done,' declared Theodore Van de Velde, 'the biological difference between masculine and feminine cannot be explained away; neither can the physical and mental contrasts between man and woman proceeding from this.' Characterized by its capacity for emotion, the feminine psyche, he declared, rendered women incapable of objectivity, of weighing the sides of an argument or of distinguishing the right and wrong of things. 'Just as her body is fashioned for maternity, so the mental quality dominating all others in the woman is motherhood.' Permanent equality in marriage, Van de Velde asserted, was abnormal because 'sexuality is always present in man and woman, and upper and lower place is inseparably allied with it.' Hostility in marriage, which was now construed as in part responsible for the disorders of contemporary life, resulted from women who sought to dominate their husbands or who struggled with them for power, he cautioned. Karl Abraham, a close colleague of Freud, described feminists as women who 'are unable to carry out a full psychical adaptation to the female sexual role,' women who, quite mistakenly, 'consider that the sex of a person has nothing to do with his or her capacities, especially in the mental field.' Even Havelock Ellis, an advocate of women's rights in the prewar period, could write that the idea that women might have 'the same education as men, the same occupations as men, even the same sports' constituted 'the source of all that was unbalanced...in the old women's movement.'[12]

Diagnoses of a 'female castration complex' or of frigidity were applied to women who ventured out of their assigned domestic, sexual sphere. Sexologist Walter Gallichan wrote in *The Poison of Prudery*, 'these degenerate women are a menace to civilisation. They provoke sex misunderstanding and antagonism; they wreck conjugal happiness.' Wilhelm Stekel agreed, insisting that 'we shall never understand the problem of the frigid woman unless we take into consideration the fact that the two sexes are engaged in a lasting conflict....dyspareunia [frigidity] is a social problem; it is one of woman's weapons in the universal struggle of the sexes.' K.A. Weith Knudsen, a Norwegian professor of jurisprudence and economics who had a large British audience, argued that this 'sexual anesthesia' 'so prevalent among civilised women' 'actually reinforces the threats to our civilisation, which in a higher degree than in any former culture is based on the assumption of mutual understanding and co-operation between the sexes.' Janet Chance, a prominent British sex reformer, stated that 'non-orgasmic' women should be kept out of politics. 'The effect of your spinster politicians, whether married or single,' she wrote, conflating, significantly, frigidity and spinsterhood, 'has yet to be analysed and made plain to the women they represent. I consider the lack of orgasm by women a fundamental question which deserves serious consideration.'[13]

French psychoanalyst Jacques Lacan, writing in the 1950s, substituted for the penis as a *sexual organ* the penis as a *symbol* of the dominance of men over women, which he termed the *phallus*. For Lacan, the oedipal crisis took place when a child learned about the sexual meanings – the rules, really – attached to various family members, accepted those meanings and rules, and took her or his place in the family system. (Or didn't accept those meanings and rules, but nevertheless had been instructed in them.) By the time the oedipal crisis ended, for Lacan, the sexuality and gender identity of the child, previously amorphous and unstable, had been fashioned according to the rules of the culture in which she or he lived. In other words, the organizing mechanism for Lacan was not a sexual organ – the penis – but the *meanings* attached to it by the culture. Having a phallus and not having a phallus meant having a different status in society, that of a 'man' or a 'woman,' with different privileges, rights, liberties, and responsibilities. The phallus represents, in Lacan's thinking, the status of men in western society, a status embraced by them and to which a number of rights are attached, chief among them the right to possess a woman. Women's lack of the status that the phallus represents induces a kind of phallus envy in them – they don't desire the actual penis itself, but the power, status, rights, and independence that the phallus symbolizes.

Object-relations theories

Some Anglophone followers of Freud rejected the intimations that 'biology is destiny' as it pertained to the development of a gendered identity and developed an aspect of Freud's thinking that centered on the child's relationship to its mother, the first 'object,' as Freud and subsequent psychoanalysts termed her, of the child's attention and feelings. (To us, the word 'object' might seem odd to apply to a figure as immediately present to us as a mother – it seems cold and impersonal. But it is meant to convey the notion of a child's 'love object.') We tend to identify two British analysts, D.W. Winnicott and Melanie Klein, with what came to be called 'object-relations theory,' the body of thought that emphasized the crucial importance of the child's relationship with its mother in its formation of identity, including gender and sexual identity.

Freud believed that the whole purpose of life, as far as human beings go, was to have their needs met. What those needs were, however, was not always clear in his writings. At some points they consisted of the satisfaction or resolution of basic instincts like hunger or pain; he called this the 'pleasure principle,' arguing that everything we do is organized around the compulsion – the drive – we feel to gain pleasure. In this rendering, the 'objects' – persons – who gratify our physical instincts don't matter all that much. After 1914, however, Freud began to introduce relationships with others – with objects – as an important aspect of the development of a child's sense of self, of identity. In these later works, the quality of the relationship the child has with others – objects – matters a great deal, as we've seen in the oedipal complex drama.

Winnicott, Klein, and other object-relations theorists regarded the child's relationship with its mother as central to both the process and the outcome of identity formation. Where Freud regarded instinctual drives and their satisfaction as autonomous, object-relations theorists argued that these could not be separated out from the objects – the people – to whom the drives were directed. The relationships the child had with the object of her or his drives gave those drives – and their satisfaction – meaning. Over the first three years of life, infants and then toddlers established their abilities to think, talk, walk, handle stress, and express and contain emotions and thoughts in relationship with their mothers. Through a process of individuation and separation from his or her mother, the child would develop into an adult capable of negotiating the world in a healthy way. *If* the mother provided 'good enough' care, as Winnicott put it, that is. With it, the child would grow up with the capacity to look for and form the same kind of relationships with others; without 'good enough' care, she or he might not only *not* be able to form good relationships with others; he or she might be saddled with any number of personality distortions associated with mental illness.

Most object-relations theorists before the 1970s did not put forward a systematic process by means of which individual children took on a gendered identity. Moreover, like Freud and Lacan, they based their theories on a particular model of family life that cannot be understood to be universal either across time or cultures or, indeed, within cultures: a bourgeois nuclear family made up of a father who went out to work and a mother who stayed at home with her children. But unlike Freud or Lacan, whose theories of gender and sexual identity finally came down to the possession or lack of a particular anatomical feature, which, presumably, could never be made different, object-relations theorists believed that human beings are social at their core. That is, they did not accept Freud's position that the sheer *physical* satisfaction of drives is enough. Instead, object-relations theorists argued that drives could not be separated out from the object of those drives; they saw in *relationships* with other human beings the essence of individual identity. Because individual identity – including gender identity – is formed in the context of these social interactions, it follows that if those social relationships were to change, so, too, could identity.

This is an idea we should hold on to.

2 'One is not born a woman': The Feminist Challenge

The above quotation comes from Simone de Beauvoir's 1949 classic, *The Second Sex*, whose seventeenth edition's blurb read, 'The first manifesto of the liberated woman.' Hardly. By the time Beauvoir wrote, a vast international feminist movement had already come and gone, and the 'second wave' of feminism was still two decades away. But it was a good sales pitch, especially in 1970, when feminists in the West were just getting going and didn't have a much understanding of what had gone before.

For a great deal *had* gone on before. For centuries, individual women had contested the misogynist characterization of their nature and tried to resist the proscriptions placed upon them. During the Renaissance, Christine de Pisan had engaged the '*Querelle des femmes*' (the argument over the nature of women) to assert that what passed for women's inferiority had been entirely fabricated by men and did not reflect the workings of nature. Seventeenth- and eighteenth-century women such as Aphra Behn and Mary Astell had done the same; and at the end of the eighteenth century, in the context of the French Revolution, Olympe de Gouges and Mary Wollstonecraft had drafted comprehensive manifestoes calling for the equality of women. Their respective *Declaration of the Rights of Woman and the Female Citizen* (1791) and *A Vindication of the Rights of Woman* (1790) galvanized later activists when feminism grew from the project of a few exceptional women into a broad-based movement.

▶ The first wave of feminism

Nineteenth-century feminist movements arose in Europe and America in response to the exclusion of women from participating in political and public life, especially as liberal and democratic regimes obtained those rights for increasing numbers of men in the eighteenth and nineteenth centuries. Women's exclusion was argued for and justified by references to their sexual differences from men, differences, it was asserted over and over again, that derived from nature. As a consequence, western feminists had to answer their opponents in the language used to categorize women as inferior. They had to refuse the ideology of sexual difference that established their inferiority as fact, to transgress the boundaries and practices that normalized 'women.'

One of the most powerful theorists of the nineteenth century, Harriet Taylor Mill, provided a theoretical foundation for the arguments feminists advanced throughout their campaign. Her 'Enfranchisement of Women,' published in the *Westminster Review* in 1851, was widely read and then circulated by the members of the Women's Suffrage Society in 1868. To Harriet Mill, John Stuart Mill attributed most of the ideas he presented in *The Subjection of Women*, published in 1869 but written eight years earlier. The Mills pointed out that the distinctions between the sexes imposed by society were purported to be those delineated by nature, that the private sphere belonged to women, and the public sphere to men, because of biological differences between the two. Separate-sphere ideology, encompassing the notion of natural differences between the sexes, justified the exclusion of women from power and reinforced and perpetuated the stereotype of women as 'the Sex,' making them vulnerable to abuse by men. As Harriet Mill noted, 'many persons think they have sufficiently justified the restrictions of women's field of action, when they have said that the pursuits from which women are excluded are *unfeminine*, and that the *proper sphere* of women is not politics or publicity, but private and domestic life.' She insisted that cultural constructions of masculinity and femininity bore no relation to the reality of male and female character, stating, 'we deny the right of any portion of the species to decide for another portion, or any individual for another individual, what is and what is not their "proper sphere." The proper sphere for all human beings is the largest and highest which they are able to attain to.'

Harriet Mill did not attempt to deny that male and female natures, as evident in her society, differed markedly. She would not, however, concede that these differences were necessarily natural or inherent to the two sexes. In the case of sexuality, for instance, she noted that 'whether nature made a difference in the nature of men and women or not, it seems now that all men, with the exception of a few lofty minds, are sensualists more or less – women on the contrary are quite exempt from this trait, however it may appear otherwise in the cases of some.' She thought that the most likely explanation for these differences derived from the socialization of boys and girls, 'that the habits of freedom and low indulgence on which boys grow up and the contrary notion of what is called purity in girls may have produced the appearance of different natures in the two sexes.' 'What is now called the nature of women is an eminently artificial thing,' insisted her husband. 'What women are is what we have required them to be.'

Harriet Mill suggested that separate-sphere ideology camouflaged and made palatable a system of unequal power relationships. The designation of 'self-will and self-assertion' as 'manly virtues,' and those of 'abnegation of self, patience, resignation, and submission to power' as 'the duties and graces required of women,' she maintained, meant in reality 'that power makes itself the centre of moral obligation, and that a man likes to have his own will, but does not like that his domestic companion should have a will different from his.' The so-called influence of women within the private sphere, stemming from their special morality and purity, Mill contended, concealed a distinct lack of power to determine their lives. 'What is wanted for women,' she declared, 'is equal rights, equal admission to all social privileges; not a position apart, a sort of sentimental priesthood.' Women's dependence upon men, John Stuart Mill argued, rendered them vulnerable to them; it produced a situation 'which in nine cases out of ten, makes her either the plaything or the slave of the man who feeds her.' He emphasized the link between power in the public sphere and that in the private sphere. He believed that society insisted upon the continued exclusion of women from public power because men feared the corresponding power that they would obtain in the private sphere. 'I believe that their disabilities elsewhere,' he stated, referring to the law of coverture, 'are clung to in order to maintain their subordination in domestic life.' Men's 'antipathy to the equal freedom of women,' he charged, concealed the real fear 'lest they should insist that marriage should be on equal conditions.'

Starting in the 1880s, marriage, one of liberalism's central institutions, without which it could not effectively exist in its classical form, sustained a wide-ranging assault from a vocal segment of British society. Domestic ideology, upon which liberalism was based, imbued marriage and motherhood with an element of the divine. Victorians and Edwardians viewed marriage as 'the equal yoking together of the man and the woman for the performance of high and sacred duties.' Marriage was the sphere in which the relations between men and women were said to be inspired by love, purity, and altruism, in marked contrast to the institution of prostitution, where greed, base sensuality, and corruption characterized male and female interaction. The deliberate refusal of a woman to marry constituted a clear sign of her intentions to defy conventional expectations of the female role. But those women who sought marriage and yet were 'left on the shelf,' as the saying went, realized some improvement in their situation. For most of the nineteenth century, they would have been regarded, and would have regarded themselves, as failures. By the 1890s, with the increase in respectable occupations available to women, judgment would not have been quite so harsh, and perhaps not so readily internalized.

The traditional, patriarchal marriage, characterized by inequality between spouses and the notion of the 'natural' subordination of the wife, remained the accepted norm throughout the Victorian and Edwardian eras. Ignorance about sex, unreliable methods of contraception, and the ever-present dangers of child-birth often meant that the intimate aspects of marriage for women could be quite unpleasant. But at least partly as a result of such reforms as the Married Women's Property Acts and the Matrimonial Causes Act of 1857, the spread of contraceptive information among the middle classes after 1876, and the feminist attack on marriage as a trade, matrimony slowly took on a new meaning, one that emphasized companionship and partnership. This trend continued with the establishment of the Royal Commission on Divorce, whose recommendations for equalization of grounds for divorce became law in 1923.

Marriage and family life produced untold happiness for vast numbers of people in Britain. But starting in the 1880s, many of the women involved in the various women's rights movements seeking to obtain property rights, education and employment opportunities, to raise the age of consent for girls, and win the vote embarked upon a campaign to expose the inequalities and iniquities of marriage. For them, marriage epitomized and helped to perpetuate the notion of the meek, submissive, powerless woman. It appeared to be 'incompatible with freedom & with an independent career,' wrote Elizabeth Garrett, one of the pioneer physicians in England, the eve of her own marriage in 1870.

The heroines of 'New Woman' novelists rejected at least some aspects of the feminine role defined by Victorians and found themselves in situations that demonstrated that marriage was not the haven depicted in conventional popular literature. Sarah Grand, for example, focused on the institution of marriage in order to expose its hypocrisy. Her characters spoke candidly and without guile about venereal disease, prostitution, and adultery, rejecting the stereotype of feminine delicacy. Other novelists questioned the institution of marriage itself. Mona Caird, for instance, in *Daughters of Danaus*, insisted that freedom for women was impossible 'without the marriage-relation, as at present understood, being called in question.' The demand for a modified marriage, whether or not intended by all those women who claimed freedom, was inherent in the feminist message, she claimed. 'The spirit of liberty among women is increasing rapidly,' she argued, 'and as soon as an approach to economic independence gives them the power to refuse, without harsh penalty, the terms which men have hitherto been able to dictate to them, in and out of marriage, we shall have some just right to call ourselves a free people.'

Feminist critics did not object to marriage in the abstract. Most of them believed that a good marriage offered opportunities for marriage that could not be found elsewhere. They condemned marriage in its present, corrupt state, arguing that the private sphere, where women's purity and special moral nature supposedly prevailed, had in fact been invaded and conquered by the destructive values and behavior of the public sphere, presided over by men. Society's understandings of male sexuality created tensions within the ideology of separate spheres, rendering it inherently contradictory and hypocritical. Challenging the prevalent ideas about marriage as 'connubial bliss,' feminists posited that marriage resembled nothing more closely than a commercial contract, in which women exchanged themselves – their legal rights, their property, their bodies, and the fruits of their labor – for a wage paid in the form of material subsistence. Barred by law and custom from entering trades and professions by which they could support themselves, and restricted in the possession of property, women had only one means of livelihood, that of marriage. Those who controlled production, declared Cicely Hamilton in her 1909 *Marriage as a Trade*, demanded of woman 'that she should enkindle and satisfy the desire of the male, who would thereupon admit her to such share of the property he possessed or earned as should seem good to him. In other words, she exchanged, by the ordinary process of barter, possession of her person for the means of subsistence.' This state of affairs, Hamilton concluded, 'justifies us in regarding marriage as essentially (from the woman's point of view) a commercial or trade undertaking.' Sanctification of marriage by the church, custom, and public opinion obscured the motives of women who sought marriage; feminists insisted that the underpinning of marriage was material. Woman 'frequently obtains a husband only in order to support life,' Hamilton claimed. 'The housekeeping trade is the only one open to us – so we enter the housekeeping trade in order to live. That is not always the same as entering the housekeeping trade in order to love.'

The marriage contract, buttressed by the laws of Britain and the United States, gave husbands complete possession of their wives' bodies. Feminists charged that the rights of husbands to force sexual intercourse and compulsory childbearing on their wives established a condition of 'sex-slavery,' as *Common Cause*, the official newspaper of the National Union of Women's Suffrage Societies, described it in 1910. For many, this issue stood at the center of the feminist movement. 'Foremost of all the wrongs from which women suffer,' declared Elizabeth Wolstenholme Elmy in 1888, 'and in itself creative of many of them, is the inequality and injustice of their position in the marriage relation, and the legal denial to wives of that personal freedom, which is the most sacred right of humanity.' Laws that taught men to regard women as their property, she asserted, permitted and encouraged 'outrages upon women, especially upon wives.' Marion Leslie wrote to the *Women's Penny Paper* in 1890 that 'so long as in the eyes of the law a woman is the property of her husband, and can be lawfully chastised by him,' men will be brutal and overbearing to women, despite the most energetically conducted palliative schemes.'

Couched in rather vague terms, the issue that so inflamed the passions of feminists was marital rape. A husband's right to sexual intercourse with his wife was absolute, superseding even the right of a woman to protect herself and/or her unborn children from disease. In the ruling handed down in *Regina v. Clarence* in 1888, the judge established the precedent that a husband could not be found guilty of raping his wife even if she had refused intercourse because he had venereal disease. Elmy denounced 'this infamy in the name of the wife, the mother, the child, the race, and the higher humanity to which we aspire.' She wrote to her friend Harriet McIlquham in 1897 that 'the making criminal in a husband the communication of foul disease to his wife' and the overturning of *Regina v. Clarence* were 'two of the first things at which we shall have to work when once we win the Suffrage, and they will carry us very far indeed.'

While Victorian theorists praised the moral, spiritual qualities of women, feminists emphasized that patriarchal society valued women only for their capacity to satisfy male sexual needs and to reproduce the race. The male design for women, Caird contended, no matter how well camouflaged and sanctified by marriage, remained 'that a woman's main duty and privilege was to bear children without limit; that death and suffering were not to be considered for a moment, in the performance of this duty; that for this end she had been created, and for this end...she must live and die.' Cicely Hamilton proclaimed that 'women have been trained to be unintelligent breeding-machines until they have become unintelligent breeding-machines.' So pervasively had the private sphere of women been taken over by the values of the public sphere of men that the terms 'woman' and 'breeding machine' had become indistinguishable, she lamented. Constraints on a woman's ability to secure a livelihood outside marriage, a legal system that gave husbands absolute control over their wives' bodies, and an ideology that insisted upon the primacy of the sexual functions of women engendered a situation in which motherhood reflected not 'the mighty creative power which more than any other human faculty seems to bring womanhood nearer the Divine,' but compulsory, forced labor. Hamilton argued that childbearing was 'an involuntary consequence of a compulsory trade.' Children 'are born of women who are not free,' Caird declared, 'not free even to refuse to bear them.'

The feminist critique of marriage necessarily involved a critique of masculinity. Male sexuality, exemplified in microcosm by the institution of marriage, was, women like Josephine Butler, Elizabeth Wolstenholme Elmy, and Frances Swiney believed, destructive both to women and ultimately to the whole of humanity. 'One of the most revolting spectacles still extant in our "civilization,"' lamented Elmy in 1896, was 'that of a husband wearing out (i.e., literally killing) his wife with child-births...with sheer licentiousness.' Swiney decried the fact that 'one fortnight after confinement some men will insist on resuming sexual relations with their wives.' Such practices led her to conclude that 'men have sought in woman only a body. They have possessed that body. They have made it the refuse heap of sexual pathology.'

The experiences of women in marriage, where, in the words of Elmy, they were subject to 'the excess of sexual proclivity and indulgence general on the part of man,' led feminists to demand the right to control their bodies and their fertility.

Yet artificial means of birth control were anathema to feminists, who believed that they would simply allow men easier and more frequent access to their wives by eliminating the fear of pregnancy. Feminists opposed contraception because they feared it would 'give men greater sexual license.' Contraceptive knowledge did not become an explicit feminist demand until after the turn of the century, and even then it only rarely found its way into print until after World War I. Feminists certainly favored 'voluntary motherhood' – the right to abstain from sexual intercourse. For some, in fact, the right to refuse intercourse stood at the core of their movement. Lady Florence Dixie announced in the *Woman's Herald* in 1891 that the feminist 'Plan of Campaign' for women prominently included 'rights over their own person and the control of the birth of children.' Elmy insisted that 'the functions of wifehood and motherhood must remain solely and entirely within the wife's own option.' But abstinence from sexual intercourse was possible only if men agreed to it, something feminists doubted the willingness of most husbands to do. Their critique of masculinity instilled in them the conviction that only a massive transformation in the laws, customs, mores, and traditions of Britain could produce a society in which women might exercise the same freedom and liberty accorded to men.

The most radical challenge of the women's movement to patriarchal control consisted of demands for enfranchisement on the same lines as men. The campaign for the vote was designed to eliminate the notions of separate spheres and 'natural' differences between the sexes insisted upon by domestic ideology, to eliminate patriarchy, and usher in a regime of equality between men and women in private as well as public life.

By the beginning of the twentieth century, suffrage campaigns in America and Europe had attained the status of mass movements. In Britain, with the advent of militancy arising out of the Women's Social and Political Union (WSPU) in 1905, the whole of the feminist movement centered around suffrage as the means by which women could free themselves from servile bondage to men. As a symbol of civic and political personality, the vote would be an effective agent in eliminating the notion of women as 'the Sex.' As an instrument of power, feminists believed – as did their adversaries – it would transform the elevating 'influence' of women into a tool with which to create a greater and truer morality among men by eliminating the distinctions between public and private spheres. They meant to use it to build a sexual culture in Britain that would reflect the needs, desires, and interests of bourgeois women. Feminists sought to eliminate the stereotypes of women – both the idealized and the feared – that rendered them inhuman and, through the weapon of the vote, to create a society that was consistent with their needs, interests, and self-defined reality. 'Votes for Women, Chastity for Men,' Christabel Pankhurst's summation of the demands of feminist women, reflected the deeply felt conviction that the regimes of male sexuality and female subordination called into being by separate-sphere ideology had to be transformed. The suffrage movement, she insisted, constituted 'a revolt against the evil system under which women are regarded as sub-human and as the sex slaves of men.'[1]

▶ Second-wave feminist critiques

In 1949, Simone de Beauvoir, a member of a philosophical group of people who called themselves existentialists, asserted in her book *The Second Sex* that 'one is not born a woman, but, rather, becomes one.' She pointed out that what appeared to be a symmetrical duality of masculine and feminine was no such thing, for in actuality men served as the 'absolute human type' against which women were positioned as the 'other.' 'Thus humanity is male and man defines woman not in herself,' she argued, 'but as relative to him; she is not regarded as an autonomous being.' She was what he defined her to be; moreover, Beauvoir declared, 'she appears essentially to the male as a sexual being. For him she is sex – absolute sex, no less.'[2] At the time no identifiable feminist movement existed that might pick up on her astute statement, but when one did appear 20 years later in Europe and the United States, the power of her thinking on this issue readily caught the attention of many women who would become feminist theorists.

What is called the second wave of feminism, known at the time as women's liberation, arose in the West in the late 1960s. Inspired in part by the civil rights movements in the United States, and the 'New Left' movements in Europe, women in Britain, France, Germany, Italy, and America began to demand freedom from the roles, portrayals, and expectations that limited, diminished, and oppressed them. The sexual revolution of the 1960s had placed a premium on men's pleasures and the fulfillment of their sexual desires at the expense of women, whose highly sexualized images appeared in magazines like *Playboy* and *Penthouse*, on billboards and posters. Women's liberation activists protested loudly and vividly against such depictions of women as sexual objects. One of their first actions took place in 1970 at the Miss World beauty contest in London, when a group of women interrupted the pageant by leaping on stage and blowing whistles, hooting, mooing like cattle, and brandishing signs that read 'Miss-conception,' 'Miss-treated,' 'Miss-placed,' and 'Miss-judged.' They lobbed stink bombs, flour bombs, and smoke bombs at the contestants, the judges, and at Bob Hope, the master of ceremonies. Their actions resembled those of the militant suffragists of the first decade of the twentieth century, and earned them the same result – arrest. They created a spectacle that succeeded in garnering for the movement enormous publicity.[3] In the United States, the National Organization for Women (NOW) mobilized a Women's Strike for Equality on August 26, 1970. Thousands of women in cities across the country showed up, carrying banners and signs demanding their rights. The visibility of the women's liberation movement increased markedly, and thousands more women flocked to join NOW and various other groups. In 1975, over 300 feminist events took place in the United States. Some 70 women's liberation groups existed in London alone by 1969. In Paris, feminist groups with names like *Psychanalyse et Politique* and *Elles Voient Rouge* ('Women See Red') formed. Publications like *MS, Shrew, Red Rag*, and *Spare Rib* appeared, analyzing women's oppression, recounting earlier feminist efforts, spreading the feminist message, and making claims for women's personal, sexual, and familial freedom.

In the United States, a presidential order making civil service jobs open to those who qualified 'without regard to sex,' the Equal Pay Act of 1963, the extension of the 1964 Title VII outlawing discrimination in employment to include 'sex,' and the passage of Title IX banning discrimination in education in 1972; and in Britain, the Equal Pay Acts of 1970 and 1975 and the Sex Discrimination Act of 1975 made it possible for women to gain equal treatment with men in some areas of education, training, and wage-earning. But 'second-wave' feminists looked for more than equality with men before the law; they sought changes in the law, the social and economic system, and the culture that would 'liberate' them from current conceptions of femininity that, they argued, locked them into stifling, unfulfilling, slavish positions, and often made them vulnerable to sexual predations from men. Unlike contemporary liberal feminists and those of the nineteenth and early twentieth centuries, feminists seeking liberation believed that the very system in which they lived required abolition or complete overhaul.

Feminists differed in their designations of just what system it was that oppressed them. Socialist feminists hailing from New Left organizations identified capitalism as the source of conditions that rendered them inferior to men. Like Marx, explained Hilary Rose, who 'was able to go behind the appearance of freedom in the labour market in which buyers and sellers freely bought and sold, to reveal the systemic relations of domination and subordination which are located within the capitalist mode of production itself,' socialist, or materialist, feminists must 'go behind – above all in personal life – the appearance of love and the naturalness of a woman's place and a woman's work, to reveal the equally systemic relationships of the sex-gender world.'[4] The family, in particular, socialist feminists argued, in which the understandings and assumptions and the labor force necessary to keep capitalism working were reproduced, required complete transformation. For socialist feminists, adherence to Marxist doctrine and to socialist groups remained a significant aspect of their politics, the goal of which was to eliminate the unjust class system produced by capitalism and reproduced by the family. The achievement of feminist aims would follow upon its extinction. At the same time, their insistence that women's work, experiences, and functions in a capitalist society could not simply be subsumed into those of men forced traditional socialists to enlarge their understandings and expand their analyses of capitalism.

Radical feminists, by contrast, saw in domination by men, in patriarchy and not in the economic system, the root of their oppression. They insisted that if women were to be liberated, they would have to arrive at a 'consciousness' of their oppression. As Dale Spender put it,

> a patriarchal society depends in large measure on the experience and values of males being perceived as the *only* valid frame of reference for society, and ... it is therefore in patriarchal interest to prevent women from sharing, establishing and asserting their equally real, valid and *different* frame of reference, which is the outcome of different experience.[5]

In 'consciousness-raising' sessions where they explored their personal lives in depth, many feminists gained an understanding of how patriarchy operated in the most insidious ways to make women complicit in their own subservience to men. In consequence, some radical feminists – many of them lesbians who had been ostracized by straight feminists who feared that their movement would be tainted by association with lesbianism – became convinced that they would ultimately have to remove themselves from sexual and social relationships with men. Separatism, as they saw it, provided the only avenue to liberation. As British feminist Amanda Sebestyn described radical feminists later,

> we wanted to leave men no matter what, we started squatting so we could live with other women, we acquired of necessity new 'male' skills of plumbing, electricity, carpentry and car maintenance, setting up our own discos and then forming bands to dance to. We cut our hair very short and stopped wearing 'women's' clothes, we stopped smiling and being 'nice.'[6]

Despite their differences, which would become increasingly evident and acrimonious in the mid- and late 1970s, feminists of virtually every stripe agreed that women's sexual freedom, their capacity to choose the kind of intimate or social grouping in which they would live, and determining for themselves the kind of work they would do, were vital to their liberation. They could readily come together to support reforms that contributed to that end: access to free and legal contraception and abortion; equal pay; health, educational, and social services; increased penalties for rape and domestic violence; nursery and day care for children; and provisions that enabled women to be legally and financially independent, such as divorce law reform and wages for housework. They made clear from the start that they intended their varieties of feminism to create entirely different roles, expectations, identities, and material realities for women than those currently operative. Their focus on personal and family issues, and on social and cultural practices – like the clubs, bookstores, magazines, and literature of the 'sexual revolution' that

gratuitously portrayed women as the proper objects of male sexual desire and violence – gave their movement a broad comprehensiveness that touched the lives of
subsequent generations of women – and men – to come.

▶ Theories of oppression[7]

Feminist theories of gender grew out of the efforts of feminist scholars in the
1970s to explain and determine the origins of women's oppression. These writers understood 'gender' to refer to the socially and culturally imposed images of
and roles for women, differentiating it from 'sex,' a biological category that locked
women into particular roles and relationships by virtue of their reproductive capacity. When they spoke of a 'sex/gender' system, they meant the human social and
cultural arrangements that were imposed on biological sexual and reproductive
processes. Many of the first theorists inserted gender into Marx's theory of historical materialism: Shulamith Firestone, for example, argued that the 'sex/gender'
system undergirded and provided the template for the inequalities inherent in
the class system under capitalism. Sex and gender inequalities, in other words,
based on the reproductive differences of men and women, both pre-dated and
required the development of the class system. She identified four 'fundamental – if not immutable – facts' that determined women's inequalities: (1) because
they bore and reared children, women depended upon men for their physical
survival; (2) infants remained dependent upon adults for their physical survival
for a long time; (3) the dependency of children upon their mothers – and the
interdependency this produced between mothers and children – has profoundly
influenced the psychology of women and children; and (4) the reproductive differences between men and women established the first division of labor that lies
at the heart of class. Putting all these 'facts' together, Firestone argued that the
relationships developed within the biological family distorted the psychosexual
characteristics of human personality.

Seeing in the biological family – the reproductive unit of male, female, and
infant – inherently unequal power relations, Firestone came close to regarding
the sex/gender system as natural, though not necessarily unchangeable. Human
beings, she noted, had for eons found ways to go beyond nature and to establish
the conditions of their lives; men had in fact escaped from the biological structures
that might have trapped them. Women, she insisted, must do the same. They must
realize that genital differences do not have the same valence culturally that they
once had: they must seize control of reproduction and child-rearing practices and
eliminate not just male privilege but sex distinction itself. By promoting pansexu-
ality, artificial reproduction, single parenthood, parenting by fathers, communal
child-raising, and the elimination of differences in physical strength by means

of new technologies and practices, Firestone claimed, the psychosocial distortions associated with the inequalities of power within the current sex/gender system – especially the aggression of men against women – would end.[8]

But as Gayle Rubin pointed out, adding gender to historical materialism might explain how women and reproduction were useful to capitalism, but failed to account for all those pre-capitalist societies that oppressed women no less than did developed capitalist societies. Rubin offered her own argument about the origins of women's oppression in 'The Traffic in Women' (1975), drawing on the work of anthropologist Claude Lévi-Strauss to argue that the exchange of women in kinship systems established the sexual division of labor, the incest taboo, and heteronormativity, which served, in virtually every society, to create profound inequalities between men and women.

It goes like this. Kinship systems, according to Lévi-Strauss and Rubin, organize sexuality and procreation and replicate them over time. They do so by creating categories and statuses for their members and for outsiders. At the heart of kinship systems lies the practice of exchanging women between men, a process of 'gifting' that establishes relationships between those men based on trust, solidarity, and mutual assistance. 'Gifting' generally and the gifting of women in particular acts as the cement, the glue, that holds societies together, that enables them to remain peaceful in the absence of governmental institutions. The exchange of women takes place through marriage, and by insisting that women marry outside their immediate groups – an insistence we call the 'incest taboo' – kin create a large network of relations across a wide range of people. The ties between these people, created by the exchange of women, constitute a kinship structure.

Here's the key. Women do not participate in the gifting; they constitute the gift itself. As a consequence, they act as the means through which relationships are established, and are not a partner in those relationships. The social linkages established through the exchange of women redound upon the partners – the men – and not upon the women, the exchanged object. Women are not partners to their husbands, they are the property of their fathers or brothers and then their husbands, and thus is the oppression of women established.

These practices were social and cultural, Rubin insisted, not biological. Just as humans required food and drink to stay alive, they required sexuality and procreation to ensure the survival of their species. But satisfying the needs of sex and reproduction turned on the same kind of social and cultural processes as did satisfying the needs of hunger and thirst. Rubin regarded the inequalities and oppression evident in the 'sex/gender' systems of past and current societies as artifacts, as products of the particular social arrangements that organized them. Oppression and inequalities of power were not inevitable, not the natural consequence of biology, sex, and reproduction. Nor were the gender differences attributed to males and females universal, as Freud and many others implied; they were a result of the particular, specific, kinship systems out of which they emerged. The task for feminists, then, Rubin asserted, consists of understanding the exact mechanisms by means of which particular conventions of sexuality are produced, maintained, and passed down.

Here Rubin turned to Lévi-Strauss's thinking about the sexual division of labor. Every society we know about divides up the work that needs doing between males and females. But it does not follow that they do so in the same way; in fact, when we look across cultures we find an endless variety of what jobs go to women and what to men. In some places, women hunted and waged war while men took care of children; in others, the tables were turned. The sexual division of labor, in other words, is itself social, and not biological. Lévi-Strauss wanted to know why, if these tasks were not assigned according to biological criteria, they had to be assigned to people of different sexes at all – what was the purpose of that? To ensure heterosexuality, he determined, by requiring that the smallest viable economic unit of any society consist of at least one man and one woman.

The sexual division of labor – that is, the apparently random assignment of certain jobs to men and certain jobs to women – operated to differentiate women from men, to create 'gender.' And it also served as a kind of taboo, Rubin claimed, against establishing sexual arrangements apart from those of at least one man and one woman. It guaranteed heterosexual marriage by ensuring that economic viability – survival – depended upon the presence of at least one man and one woman. Two women or two men wouldn't do it – the tasks of production necessary to keep a household afloat could not be accomplished; only half of them would be done under a sexual division of labor system. Thus, said Rubin, we find in kinship systems, with their exchange of women and the taboos against incest and for the sexual division of labor, the rules and relations that suppress homosexuality and oppress women and homosexuals.

That's all very well, you might say, but weren't Lévi-Strauss and Rubin talking about prehistoric societies? What about their own societies of the mid- and late twentieth century? How do the practices of kinship they identified for so long ago get reproduced in the present, now that families don't serve as the economic and political institutions they once had to be? To answer that question, Rubin looked to psychoanalysis, seeing in some of Freud's formulations the means of explaining how the gender and sexual identities thrown up by western society are produced and women are subordinated. As might be expected in someone who attributes gender differences to society and culture rather than biology, she rejected Freud's ahistoricism and his later emphasis on biology in determining gender and sexual identity. Instead she relied on Lacan's gloss on Freud's oedipal theory to explain how the norms of masculinity and femininity were passed down to subsequent generations of girls and boys, an approach that removed the sexual organs as the source of difference from Freud's explanations and replaced them with theories of meanings systems about how we transmit information about sexual difference and acculturate it in our children.

▶ Feminist critiques of psychoanalysis

As Rubin pointed out, psychoanalytic theories of femininity tell a tale about the development of females that incorporates an awful lot of hurt and humiliation. In return for renouncing his mother (albeit out of fear), the boy gains the status accorded the phallus, and will by right possess a woman in the future, though not his mother. The girl, by contrast, must give up the right to her mother and, by extension, all females, since she does not possess the phallus that confers that right upon her. Angered and disappointed by her mother's lack, the girl turns to the father, the only figure who can give her the phallus she lacks. But not as he has given it to the boy. Indeed, she can only have the phallus in the sense that having been given in gift exchange to a man, she bears a male child, who bears the phallus himself. She never gets it herself, and she can never give it away. No fun.

This involves a lot of renunciation on the part of girls and the recognition that they are lacking and inferior. Moreover, they must reorient the object of their love and desire – their libido – to a different figure altogether, a man, which may well be a powerfully wrenching experience. To conform and to win the love of a new object who possesses the phallus they must become passive. They have to be tamed, domesticated, in effect. Boys don't. They simply move on to other females beyond their mother, their libidinal choice, and their phallus, intact.

Rubin found hope precisely in the fact that these processes, destructive as they may be to women and to men who did not successfully negotiate the oedipal crisis, derive from culture, not from biology. For we don't have to maintain the valuation we have bestowed upon the status of 'man' and 'woman'; we don't have to insist upon heteronormativity and conform to prescribed gender roles. We can create a society in which, as she puts it, 'one's sexual anatomy is irrelevant to who one is, what one does, and with whom one makes love.'[9]

Other feminists followed Rubin, developing by means of their criticisms, perspective, and approaches a rich and complex body of gender theory. One promising avenue derived from object-relations theory as we saw it put forward by Winnicott and Klein in the previous chapter. In 1978 Nancy Chodorow, in *The Reproduction of Mothering: Psychoanalysis and the Sociology of Gender*, offered a version of object-relations theory to explain not simply how gender identity is formed but why male-dominant gender relations persist over generations. In so doing, she addressed what she saw as the inability of men in our societies to form emotional relationships, at least compared with women, whom she saw as especially able to form emotional relationships with people, particularly other women.

Chodorow credited this difference in the emotional capabilities of men and women to the unfolding of the oedipal crisis, seeing it through the lens of object-relations theory. Like Freud, she held that mothers are the first love object for infant boys and girls. But unlike Freud, and with Winnicott and Klein, she held that the pre-oedipal relationship infants have with their mothers creates both terror and bliss. Because they are unable to differentiate themselves from their mothers – that is, they experience everything narcissistically, as being part and parcel of themselves – they luxuriate in the oneness with their mother. But as infants grow older, that oneness with mom, the utter dependence of the child on the mother, also creates a sense of loss of self, which can be a very scary feeling. The relationship of infants and toddlers with their fathers, by contrast, has from the very start contained a kind of distance; that wonderful/awful feeling of oneness has never existed with fathers, owing to the different role they play in the family. Because fathers are relatively unavailable to the infant, both physically and emotionally – they're at work, busy with guy things like mowing the lawn and fixing the car – by the time children become aware of them, fathers have always been separate beings. And babies have never felt dependent upon them, in either the terrific or terrifying aspect of the sensation. Love for a father, in other words, doesn't contain either the threat to autonomy and selfhood that love for the mother does, or the promise of a return to the blissful oneness with the mother, because the infant never had that pre-oedipal attachment to fathers that they did with mothers.

Then comes the crisis. Boys have to turn the libidinal feelings they've had for their mother to another woman, but since both 'objects' of their love are (or will be, presumably) women, the process of developing a heterosexual orientation is pretty smooth. Not so for girls, for they have to transfer their libidinal energies from their first love object, a woman, to a man if they are to take on a heterosexual identity. It's not easy, says Chodorow, and not complete: a girl's original attachment to her mother never goes away, and because her father is kind of detached emotionally, she never forms an exclusive emotional bond with him. There isn't that promise or threat of a renewed oneness with the father. Instead, she possesses an emotional tie to both mother and father, which will have an impact on the kinds of relationships she forms as an adult.

The presence of the father does help the girl to break that primal attachment she feels for her mother, and for relief of that scary feeling such dependence has engendered, the girl idealizes him. But him as a figure, not a known presence, for he's never really been that to her. He exists for her through his relationship with her mother, which means that she doesn't really know him for himself; she hasn't experienced his true personality, with all the positives and negatives that includes. She needs him for the separateness from her mother he provides, and for the kind of specialness he can make her feel, but her relationship with him is based on fantasy and idealization. In actuality, he's distant, but she's willing to accept that, as long as she can sustain the belief that he loves her. When she grows into adulthood, her relationships with men will be similar. That is, she will accept relationships with men that are not primarily emotionally based, as long as she can convince herself that they love her.

Girls also, according to Chodorow, resolve their oedipal crisis later in life than boys. Because she is a bit older, she is more likely to have a more concrete sense of self than a boy does. Her oedipal love for her father isn't as threatening as is the boy's oedipal love for his mother; the combination of a stronger sense of self and a lesser threat mean that girls have less compulsion to resolve their oedipal crisis as thoroughly as boys do. She keeps some of her emotional ties to her original love object, in other words, in a way that boys don't. Boys have to repress their oedipal love for their mothers and their intense pre-oedipal relationship with them. And because the girl still retains remnants of her pre-oedipal love for her mother, she continues to seek them as an adult. She finds these emotional ties from children and other women, rather than from men, who 'tend to remain emotionally secondary' for women, Chodorow argued. Men continually have to repress their oedipal love for their mothers who appear in the guise of adult women; the threat to autonomous selfhood posed by love is far too great. So they dismiss emotion and try to deny that they need love. Their relationships with women tend to be erotically rather than emotionally based, and carry with them the tendency to disdain the creatures, women, who express their needs for emotion and love so willingly. They deny their need for love by controlling women, and turn outward from the affective life of the family to the world of work. That, she said, had to change, and the way to change it would be to involve men much more heavily in child-rearing practices.

If you grew up in the 1950s and 1960s in a middle-class home, the situations Chodorow describes might ring true. But not all – or even most – of us did: our mothers may have worked and left us in the care of others; our fathers may not even have been there. In which case, the dynamics we saw and experienced may well have been entirely different. Moreover, Chodorow's theories about child-rearing practices, even in the homes for which they are accurate representations, don't explain why it is that women have those responsibilities in the first place. She's describing the consequences of those child-rearing practices, in other words, not offering an explanation of how they came to be in the first place. She's claiming as *causal* the social arrangements that are themselves in need of explication: why do societies assign certain roles and responsibilities to women and others to men? Why do we arrange ourselves along these lines? Why is gender – the ideas we attach to sexual difference – so persistent and prevalent a feature in our societies?

Some feminist theorists claimed that gender operates as omnipresently as it does precisely because women and men are so fundamentally different from one another psychologically. Two particularly influential theorists of difference, Hélène Cixous and Luce Irigaray, drew upon Lacan's ideas about the unconscious being structured like a language to claim that the private, emotional life of women, and the public, oppressed situation of women derive from essentially the same source. That is, they asserted, society has the power to oppress, silence, or render women invisible precisely by repressing their expression of pleasure, especially sexual pleasure – or *jouissance*, as they put it in French. Cixous and Irigaray contended, with Chodorow, that girls remain bonded with their mothers far longer than boys, and that in consequence, as they grow into women, their selves retain a fluidity that men's do not. They interrelate with others far more than men, and their sensation of the body – their physical body – is much more immediate and direct than that of men, who tend to separate their sense of self from bodily experience. Moreover, where men's pleasure focuses on one sexual organ with a single aim – orgasmic release – women's pleasure is multifocal: a variety of bodily sites produce *jouissance*. These differences, Cixous and Irigaray argued, make it impossible for women to express their sexuality within the confines of patriarchal culture, which they characterize as phallocentric, organized around men's domination of women, and logocentric. Phallocentric you probably get, but logocentric? What does that mean? Well, according to feminist theorists of difference, it is the tendency of masculine thinking, writing, expression, and language to organize itself according to binaries. Another piece of jargon, you say, and you're right. Let's put it this way: we make meaning by establishing opposites, or binary oppositions. We know what is night because it is not day; we know what is black because it is not white; we know what is male because it is not female. These binary oppositions – logocentrism – structure our ability to communicate with one another, and they are intimately tied to phallocentrism, the law of the phallus as Lacan posited it. Knowledge and communication, in other words, are themselves male-dominated, and women cannot truly know themselves within this culture. They are what men – phallocentric, logocentric culture and society – have insisted they be. So, said Cixous and Irigaray, women must purposefully explore their differences from men, celebrate them for what they are in and of themselves, and employ 'feminine' writing to articulate their pleasures and their distinct sense of self. Women are different, period, full stop. We should acknowledge these differences and validate women's experiences rather than see them as 'other,' a problem that needs to be addressed. Women should not strive to be equal with men, for that would make them unlike themselves. And what women are is just fine.

More importantly, the mobilization of women's pleasure in 'feminine' writing will expose masculine discourse for what it is: not the universal, disinterested, standard default mode of expression, but a particular form of it that operates by excluding fully half of the world. Introducing 'feminine' writing would cause logocentrism – and phallocentrism – to disintegrate into a multiplicity of discourses; it would destroy its capacity to posit itself as the unitary organizing feature of social, cultural, economic, and psychological life.

The American version of this kind of thinking stressed not women's pleasure as the source of difference, but their greater moral capacity. Carol Gilligan's *In a Different Voice* (1982) urged that girls – and later, women – demonstrate far more concern about relating with other people than do boys and then men. Boys, she argued in her critique of the male-centered moral development theory propounded by Freud, Erik Erikson, and her mentor, Lawrence Kohlberg, operated according to a set of rules that, they believed, ensured that justice would be done. As long as one played by the rules, all was well. Girls, by contrast, often eschewed the rule-governed format for one that emphasized the wellbeing of the players. They cared more for people than for the rules, in other words. Boys cared more about the rules than the people. The conclusion she drew emphasized the greater relatedness and capacity for caring among women, and the less pronounced ability, even incapacity, in men to develop an ethic of care. Their ethic focused on justice. Women worried more about taking care of others; men worried more about complying with the rules. Women differed profoundly from men, and, one could read between the lines, were more moral than men. Whether that essential difference derived from biology or from culture, it seemed inescapable.

▶ Challenges to white, middle-class feminism

Hold on, protested women of color in Britain and the United States, who found themselves in a no-win situation in the late 1960s and early 1970s. Disconcerted by their treatment at the hands of the male-dominated black power movement, yet finding women's liberation and feminism entirely irrelevant and blind to their needs and desires – 'basically a family quarrel between White women and White men,' as one African American woman put it – women of color began to form their own organizations to gain liberation for themselves.[10] In Britain Iyamide Hazeley graphically laid out the grievances black women felt within black power organizations in a poem called 'Political Union.' She observed,

> You call me 'Sister' Brother, yet I know
> that it is simply a psychological lever to prise apart
> my legs.
> 'Sister, make coffee for the movement,
> Sister, make babies for the struggle.'
> You raped my consciousness with your body
> my body with reason,
> and assuage your unconscious guilt by oral politicking
> make believing
> 'Sister, Sister.'[11]

In the United States, writers such as Alice Walker, Audre Lorde, Toni Morrison, and Angela Davis began to articulate the complicated intersections of gender, race, and sexuality in their lives and communities.

When they looked toward white feminist groups, black women saw a political program that addressed few of their concerns. 'We felt they had different priorities to us,' remarked one who was instrumental in forming the Brixton Black Women's Group in 1973.

> At that time, for example, abortion was the number one issue, and groups like Wages for Housework were making a lot of noise, too. These were hardly burning issues for us – in fact they seemed like middle-class preoccupations. To begin with, abortion wasn't something we had any problems getting as black women – it was the very reverse for us! And as for wages for housework, we were more interested in getting properly paid for the work we were doing outside the home as night cleaners, and in campaigning for more childcare facilities for black women workers.[12]

In order to deal with a dual oppression arising from racism and sexism, a number of women formed other local Black Women's Groups throughout London and in cities like Leicester, Manchester, Liverpool, Sheffield, and Nottingham. Coalitions of women of color such as the Organization of Women of Asian and African Descent (OWAAD) enabled a broader national movement to emerge within which issues of racism and sexism that concerned women of color could be addressed and a national dialogue established.

As Hazel Carby noted in a hard-hitting article, the structures of racism meant that black women experienced different kinds of subjection than white women. What white women regarded as an oppressive institution – the family – black women often found to be a place from which to resist political and cultural forms of racism. White radical feminists might espouse separatism from men; black women relied on 'progressive' men in their struggles for equality and justice. 'Our situation as Black people necessitates that we have solidarity around the fact of race, which white women of course do not need to have with white men, unless it is their negative solidarity as racial oppressors.' White feminists, Carby argued, had not recognized their role in continuing imperialist and colonialist regimes around the world, or indeed, in acting as oppressors of black people at home, and if they did, they refused to acknowledge their complicity for fear 'that this will be at the expense of concentrating upon being oppressed.'[13] Carby's critique of white women's feminism raised profoundly uncomfortable issues for many women, and it ultimately served to open up feminism as a whole to the existence of diversity in women's lives that compelled the development of far more sophisticated understandings of gender through postmodern analyses than either socialist or radical feminism had been able to provide.

Part II
Gender History

3 The Road to 'Gender'

Gender history grew out of women's history. In what follows, it may seem as if women's and gender history are not just different things altogether, but that one – gender – in flowing from the other – women – superseded it. That's only because of the order I am going to impose on the material. Remember in the Introduction, when I said that there isn't any 'past' out there for us to faithfully recover? Well, here's a perfect example of that: my choices about what to include in this chapter will create a narrative – tell a story – that appears seamless and complete. Let me assure you that it is not. Others would choose different characters and different turning points; they'd focus on different subjects; and as a result, they'd tell it differently. My version tries to be accurate in its representations, but it is made up of how I see the process unfolding, not necessarily how everyone sees it, and you need to know that up front.

Women's and gender history do indeed have much in common with one another. Women's historians study women as *subjects*, and have been doing so for a very long time, at least since the Renaissance.[1] Gender historians study the *relationship* of women to men in the context of various societies, paying particular attention to the interplay of male and female identities. Both of these sets of practitioners address subjects and use methods that overlap with one another, and women's and gender histories inform one another as a matter of course. It's not that gender history is better than women's history, or vice versa, although, as you'll also see in the next chapter, the debates that grew up between them certainly suggested that that was so. In fact, neither women's nor gender historians could do what we do these days without the other. Not only are they historically linked, but without women's history, no gender history would have been possible. Gender history depends heavily on women's history for the material it analyzes; and women's history could only provide a partial view of women's lives if it did not take gender – the interrelationships of male and female – into account.

▶ 'Hidden from history': recuperating women for history

The decade of the 1960s spawned the emergence of protests against and radical challenges to the status quo in the West. In western Europe and the English-speaking countries, New Left, civil rights, antiwar, and then, when women found themselves largely unwelcome in these groups, feminist movements sprang up, issuing calls for dramatic changes in virtually every realm across their societies. The demands for change found especial resonance within colleges and universities, formerly the repository of elite persons and of a pedagogy that perpetuated their values. The influx of non-elite white men and women and people of color into post-secondary educational institutions transformed the humanities and social science disciplines within a short period of time, and ultimately reached the natural and physical sciences as well. History departments, the object of our concern, felt the impact immediately, as calls for a 'new social history' that would focus on the lives of ordinary people rather than on the exploits of an elite few led to the development of a vital and burgeoning new sub-field. Initially it seemed to many women that the new social history would provide just the place for the lives of women to be explored as well. That didn't happen. In fact, many of the radical historians and the histories they wrote exhibited the same kinds of misogyny and discrimination against women that earlier generations of historians had practiced.

The women's liberation movements of the 1970s galvanized an entire generation of feminist historians across the western world. These brave souls – you have to imagine how hard it might have been for a lone woman in a department consisting otherwise entirely of men to challenge their practices – insisted not only that women should not have to deal with the often crippling discrimination against them but that the histories being written should include women in them. Some of the earliest works produced by these women carried titles like *Hidden from History* (1973) and *Becoming Visible* (1977), testimony to the overriding need to bring women in the past into the spotlight, to resurrect them from posterity so that they might serve as role models for the present and future. In Australia, for example, a number of biographies treating a variety of white women appeared; in the United States, women who had participated in the abolitionist, feminist, and social welfare campaigns found their historians. In Britain, feminist historians influenced by Marxist historiography tended to focus on the lives of 'ordinary' rather than elite women; while in France, women's histories drew upon the anthropological traditions of the *Annales* school and treated cultural themes that bore on women like sexuality or motherhood.[2]

The search for women's past rested in large part on two related assumptions: first, that if women were to be regarded as historical actors, historians would have to regard them as partaking of a collective identity; and secondly, a conviction that women shared a collective set of experiences on the basis of which they formed a collective identity. Women's historians, feminists themselves in virtually every instance, shared the underlying belief in much of feminist thinking that women, as both subject and object of feminism's program, share common natures, common needs, common wants, common desires, and a common oppression. Their histories sought to uncover these aspects of women's lives, and their earliest efforts at theorizing tried to explain how that oppression operated.

The outpouring of feminist histories of women stimulated the establishment of the Berkshire Conference on the History of Women in the United States, the first meeting of which was held at Douglass College, Rutgers University, in 1973. Conveners expected maybe a hundred people, but 300 showed up; another conference was planned for the following year at Radcliffe College, where over 1000 women participated. Having grown so large, the conference could not be held every year, so members decided that it would meet every three years instead, and thus Berkshire conferences met at Bryn Mawr in 1976, Mount Holyoke in 1978, Vassar in 1981, Smith in 1984, Wellesley in 1987, Douglass again in 1990, and Vassar again in 1993. With participants from all over the world, men and women alike, now reaching into the many thousands, the small women's colleges of the US east coast could no longer accommodate such crowds, and beginning in 1996, 'the Berks,' as it was called, was relocated to larger universities across the country (North Carolina, California, Connecticut, Minnesota, Massachusetts).

The successes of the Berkshire Conferences spoke unmistakably of the immense energies unleashed by women's historians. The conferences themselves, along with a number of historical journals dedicated to the study of women that emerged in the 1970s and 1980s in Britain, Australia, and the United States, also served as the sites where some of the most contentious, exciting, and fruitful debates taking place within women's history were aired. One of the earliest of those debates concerned the notion of 'patriarchy' – literally, 'rule of the father' – to explain the systems and means by which men dominate and exploit women. Depending upon their orientation, historians turned to the theories we laid out in the preceding chapter, incorporating analyses of kinship systems, capitalism, or psychoanalysis to advance their arguments.

Much good work came out of these efforts, but patriarchy as a theory tended to become ahistorical – that is, it reduced to a single cause all of women's oppression without allowing for alliances between men and women, change over time or place, or women's resistance to it. It became a monolithic force, this power derived from biological difference, suggesting that men and women were forever and everywhere locked in antagonism to one another. Sheila Rowbotham made this argument in a 1979 forum in *The New Statesman*, in which she and responders Sally Alexander and Barbara Taylor debated the relative merits of the concept. Alexander and Taylor countered that patriarchy need not be viewed as biologically based, and therefore as an unchanging entity. But more importantly, they insisted, the concept provided a theoretical framework within which women's lives could be examined and analyzed. Patriarchy served as a vital tool for historians of women, they urged, for 'history only answers questions which are put to it.' Judith Bennett added both strength and nuance to the argument in favor of patriarchy as 'feminism's central theoretical problematic' when she observed that the system that oppressed women was not exclusively that of 'male oppressor/female victim.' Men weren't only oppressors, women only victims. Rather, she pointed out, 'women...have also colluded in, undermined and survived patriarchy.'[3]

One aspect of western patriarchal systems, at least, took on enormous significance in the work of women's historians over the next 30 years or so – that of 'separate spheres' for men and women. In one of its earliest iterations, Barbara Welter regarded the private sphere of home and family for American women as a veritable prison, locking them into a domestic role that demeaned and devalued them and even made them ill.[4] In 1975, Carroll Smith-Rosenberg published one of her most famous essays, 'The Female World of Love and Ritual,' in which she turned Welter's position on its head by bringing the most cherished principles of the feminist movement – 'the personal is political' – to bear on her subjects. Rather than seeing the private sphere of home and family as an entirely negative space and place for women, Smith-Rosenberg posited it as the site where positive bonds between women were forged. Sharing the private, personal experiences of marriage, childbirth, child-rearing, religion, and family life, the women in the nineteenth-century American home developed a distinctly female culture from which men were absent. This shared, female-only culture fostered in women a sense of worth and a belief in themselves; it empowered them, in other words, rather than oppressed them, as Welter had claimed.[5] Subsequent historians expanded upon this new valorization of women's distinct culture to explain how and why women ventured out from their private sphere to engage in social and political reform activities in the public realm. Nancy Cott's 1977 *The Bonds of Womanhood: Woman's Sphere in New England, 1780–1835*, was followed by Blanche Wiesen Cook's 'Female Support Networks and Political Activism: Lillian Wald, Crystal Eastman, Emma Goldman' (1979), Estelle Freeman's 'Separatism as Strategy: Female Institution Building and American Feminism' (1979); Nancy Sahli's 'Smashing: Women's Relationships Before the Fall' (1979), Mary Ryan's 'The Power of Women's Networks' (1983), and Kitty Sklar's 'Hull House in the 1980s: A Community of Women Reformers' (1985).

The strengths of this approach were many. First, it brought to light the activities of women in a wide array of both private and public activities that conventional histories simply ignored. It tied the personal to the political, showing how public, political activity arose from the experiences of private life. And it demonstrated just how historical entities like sex and gender were – that is, that they were not static categories, but changed over time. But although the models of separate spheres and of a distinct women's culture proved long-lasting in women's history, they were not without their critics. In the United States in 1980, Ellen DuBois decried the depoliticising of feminist history, as she saw it, that the emphasis on women's culture brought about. Others pointed out that the separate sphere that produced a distinctly female culture could not be said to apply to the lives of working women or women of color, or of many groups outside of America.

Another group of women's historians turned to the practices developed within the 'new social history' to bring women into history. Because social history emphasized not great men as the movers and shakers of history, but focused on large societal processes such as the development of capitalism; because it set its sights on such non-traditional subjects as family relationships, fertility, demography, and sexuality, and borrowed heavily from a number of disciplines in order to study them; and because it legitimated the study of groups not normally found in history books – peasants, slaves, workers, for example – the field looked to be a promising site for the entry of women onto its terrains. As indeed it was: the studies done by women's historians resist counting at this point; suffice it to say that many, many hundreds of articles and books appeared in which the lives of women figured prominently.

▶ Gender

But as Joan Scott pointed out in 1983, neither the women's culture nor the social history approach had the effect its practitioners had sought – to rewrite conventional history as it had been practiced in the West for the past 100 years. The first, she argued, while replacing men with women as the subject of historical study, nonetheless continued to separate women out from history as traditionally written. The second – adding women to social history – didn't change the story that social history told. Social history may well have rewritten conventional political history, but the addition of women to it had not made an appreciable difference. 'Women are a department of social history,' Scott pointed out, too integrated within it to offer productive insights or provocative questions. The solution, she suggested, for feminist historians who hoped to transform history as a practice was to incorporate 'gender' into their studies, an analytic category that derived from and expanded upon the abundance of studies already produced by historians of women.[6]

Scott was certainly not the first to introduce the concept of gender. In the 1970s, two historians, Joan Kelly and Natalie Zemon Davis, began to call for a new approach to women's history that implied, if they did not always explicitly utilize, the term. Rather than try to study women in isolation from men, they argued, women's historians needed to study them in relation to men. At the 1975 Berkshire Conference, Davis told her audience

> that we should be interested in the history of both women and men, that we should not be working only on the subjected sex any more than an historian of class can focus exclusively on peasants. Our goal is to understand the significance of the *sexes*, of gender groups in the historical past. Our goal is to discover the range in sex roles and in sexual symbolism in different societies and periods, to find out what meaning they had and how they functioned to maintain the social order or to promote its change.[7]

She believed that such an approach, which we would identify as a gendered history, promised to compel whole new ways of thinking about many of the issues that concerned historians – power, social structure, property, symbols, and periodization.

Davis's call resonated with Joan Kelly, who had been thinking along the same lines already. Her 1976 *Signs* article, 'The Social Relations of the Sexes', echoed Davis in claiming that 'the activity, power, and cultural evaluation of women simply cannot be assessed except in relational terms: by comparison and contrast with the activity, power, and cultural evaluation of men, and in relation to the institutions and social developments that shape the sexual order.'[8] Davis and Kelly asserted not only that placing women in relation to men enabled historians to understand women more comprehensively, but it placed gender – the relations of the sexes – smack in the center of any study of society. It would no longer be possible, they were confident, to study society and its many institutions and offshoots without incorporating gender.

By 1985, *History Workshop*, the British socialist journal established in 1976 as an outlet for scholarship carried out outside of Britain's conservative history departments, had arrived at much the same conclusion. It noted that 'while rediscovering the worlds that women have inhabited is important ... it can lead to a ghettoisation of women's history and to its presentation in forms which historians working in different fields find easy to ignore.' It urged feminists to continue to write women's histories, but to include in their works the 'reconstructing of men as social group and gender category [*sic*]' so that a fuller reading of the historical record might be possible.[9]

In one of the most influential treatments utilizing gender, *Family Fortunes: Men and Women of the English Middle Class* (1987), Leonore Davidoff and Catherine Hall sought to demonstrate how gender stood at the very core of class identity, how it organized and structured middle-class society in Britain. At the core of their arguments stood the practice of separate spheres for men and women, which, they claimed, functioned to provide both an individual identity for men and women and a social identity for the class they were a part of creating. An arrangement in which men went out to work while their wives remained at home to maintain a decent, moral, disciplined, and well-regulated domestic life – these, in the minds of evangelicals and political economists, provided the building blocks upon which a stable, hierarchical, deferential social order could be constructed and sustained in the midst of industrial transformation and political revolution. And the families that could afford to adopt this system, who would become the bourgeois middle class of industrial Britain, drew upon the qualities they saw as inherent in it to distinguish themselves from the aristocracy above them and the working people below them. Class identity, thus, was founded upon gender.

Family Fortunes took off in the Anglophone world, garnering a broad audience and deep appreciation for its detailed, comprehensive, and innovative effort to tie gender to class formation. But it also generated a fair bit of criticism. In Britain, Amanda Vickery noted that historians' conflation of the *prescriptions* put forth by separate-sphere ideology with the *actual behavior* of men and women had grievously distorted the picture. Public and private realms never fully contained their putative inmates: men regularly and habitually acted and participated in the private sphere of home and family; women engaged in civic, political, and social activities that took them far outside the home. The book also tended to paint the relationships of men and women within the framework of separate spheres as harmonious and unproblematic, ignoring the inequalities of power that were inherent in it. These critiques ultimately took their toll on separate spheres as the dominant trope of women's history, though they never fully dislodged it, especially in Italian and German scholarship, which continues to utilize it heavily to this day.[10]

In 1986, Joan Scott published the article that would inform virtually all scholarship on gender from that moment on, 'Gender: A Useful Category of Historical Analysis.' I was in the audience the night she gave her first presentation of the paper, in December 1985 at the American Historical Association's Annual Meeting. Not many of us could grasp fully what she laid out in her talk, but I would guess that nearly all of us knew that something powerful was taking place. As it turned out, Scott's article aroused heated controversy among historians, generating fierce debate between those who found her use of postmodern theories exciting and full of possibilities, and those who saw it as a threat to the very existence of feminist history and even feminism itself.

Scott set out to find a useable theory for historians of gender. Current theories about gender, she argued, just couldn't work for historians, for whether they posited a materialist analysis of patriarchy like Shulamith Firestone's, a marrying of Marxism with feminism, an anthropological explanation like Gayle Rubin's, or a psychoanalytic theory such as Jacques Lacan's, Nancy Chodorow's, or Carol Gilligan's, they limited our capacity to incorporate differences based on race, class, or culture or to trace change over time. 'The challenge,' she pointed out, 'was to reconcile theory, which was framed in general or universal terms, and history, which was committed to the study of contextual specificity and fundamental change.'[11]

Those who tried to find an explanation for patriarchy, Scott noted, had placed gender at the center of their analyses of all social organization, and in doing so had brought to our attention important inequalities between men and women. They had not, however, been able to show how inequalities of gender worked to organize social life or how gender made an impact on realms of our existence that seemed not to have any relationship with it, such as politics or war. Moreover, the reliance on physical sexual difference to put forward these explanations tended to imply a universality and naturalness of the body that gave it – and therefore gender – an unchanging, inherent meaning. Gender became inaccessible to history in the sense that it never changed across cultures or over time. Put another way, history could only describe the ways different cultures and different societies dealt with gender inequalities that were fixed by the physical differences of men and women. Boring.

Within a Marxist tradition, gender, Scott argued, lost its ability to serve as any kind of analytic category, for it was always subsumed within the processes of dialectical materialism. That is, economic systems determined gender relationships and gender roles, and in this way of thinking, although economic systems change over time (in Marx's formulation, from feudalism, to capitalism, to socialism), gender ends up being a result, a consequence, of those changes.

In taking on psychoanalysis, Scott differentiated between the Anglo-American embrace of object-relations theory and the French preference for Lacanian analysis. Object-relations theorists, she cautioned, relied too literally on the small, concrete interactions of children with their parents to produce their explanations for gender identity and to open up possibilities for change. Limited to the family within the household, object-relations theories offered no means of tying the concept of gender or the individual person to larger social, economic, or political structures in which power resided. In focusing on the asymmetries produced by parent–child interactions, these theories neglected to discuss the issue of inequalities between men and women. How, Scott asked, can we account for the ongoing, seemingly ever-present association of masculinity with power, and the greater value consistently placed on men than women? How do children learn that men are powerful and women weak; that men are worth more than women?

We cannot understand these vital aspects of taking on gender identity, she asserted, unless we pay attention to the ways various cultures and societies represent gender; how they use gender to make evident the rules of social interaction; how they enable us to make meaning out of our experiences. Here she found Lacan's interpretation of Freud helpful, though his thinking, too, was not without its problems for historians. Think back again to our treatment of Lacan – to his stress on the key role played by language in the creation of gender identity. Lacan argued that the unconscious is structured like a language; where Freud saw infants taking on gender identity through the oedipal conflict, Lacan regarded the process as occurring when the child left what he called the 'imaginary' realm (an unconscious space of bisexual impulses unmediated by the existence of language, laws, institutions, or social processes) to enter into the conscious 'symbolic' realm of society, structured by gender norms, laws, institutions, and processes.

Lacan adopted poststructuralists' ideas about language – by which they mean systems of meaning, symbolic orders, not merely words, speech, or writing – to assert that children learn a gender identity on the basis of their relationship to the phallus. The phallus stands as the *metaphor* for sexual difference, and the threat of castration serves as the symbol of the (father's) law. The child imagines an identification with masculinity or femininity based upon his or her relationship to the phallus, and fantasizes a relationship to the law, or the rules of society, on the same basis. Because the male and female child have necessarily different relationships with the phallus, the rules of society are gendered from the start.

This sounds like absolute, unchanging sexual difference, again, doesn't it? What is different in Lacan's thinking is that although gender identity seems fixed and coherent, it is not. It's very unstable, in fact, he argued, here again using poststructuralism to make his case. We need to back up a little bit in order to understand this, to explain the structuralism that then becomes *post*structuralism, and then relate it to Lacan.

Structuralism[12] derives from semiotic analysis, that is, the linguistic practice of the analysis of signs. It is based on the idea that words in a language are *arbitrary* and *relative*, that there is no innate connection between a word and the thing to which it refers. The spoken sound 'cat' is simply a sound. We've assigned it to a furry, four-legged creature, but we could just as easily have called it something else – '*gato*,' for instance. That's the arbitrary part of it. The *relative* part posits that 'cat' gets its meaning *relative* to the other words in the closed system that is a language. That is, we assign meaning to 'cat' by understanding that it is not 'bat' or 'rat' or 'mat.' Nor is it 'car' or 'cab' or 'cap.' Nor is it 'cut' or 'cot.' 'Cat' takes on meaning only in a closed system, in this case, the English language, which (like all languages) is full of little segments of sound, able to be combined in a nearly infinite variety of patterns.

Structural linguists asked themselves how words like 'cat' functioned in our communication. They split up a word like 'cat' into two functioning parts: a *signifier* and a *signified*. The spoken word 'cat' is the *signifier*. The idea that comes into your mind (furry, four-legged, not dog) when you hear the word is the thing that is *signified*. When you take these two functions and put them together, you have the communicative act we call a *sign*. Semiotics, then, deals with the meanings that come together in the form of signifiers and signifieds to form signs. Think of a sign not as a thing, but as an act or a near-instantaneous moment of process.

Structuralists argue that the meaning of words in a language is purely arbitrary. That is to say, there is no reason why we call a large, green leafy thing a 'tree' rather than a 'snarompf.' Signs only get their meaning relative to other words in a finite language system, not because there is any direct correspondence between the word (the signifier) and the thing it stands for (the signified). The meaning of signs is not intrinsic, in other words, but relative; signs get their meaning on the basis of their difference from all the other signs in a language chain. This insight – that *meaning is relative to that which surrounds it in a closed system* – powered the semiotic analyses of the linguist Ferdinand de Saussure, the ideological analyses of the literary theorist Roland Barthes, and the narrative and social analyses of the anthropologist Claude Lévi-Strauss, among others. Lévi-Strauss and Saussure, the two great figures in the history of structuralist analysis, would go much further. They would argue that language (in the case of Saussure) and narrative (in the case of Lévi-Strauss) do not *represent* meaning so much as they create it. That is, as humans, we *only* see the world through the structures we create, namely language and – in Lévi-Strauss's adaptation – social behaviors, institutions, and stories, which he tried to see in linguistic terms. Here, Lévi-Strauss's suggestion that 'classificatory systems' operate as 'systems of meaning' translates into the conviction that we literally create meaning as we categorize our world. Simple dualisms – good/bad; old/new; ours/theirs – function as categories that structure the ways we perceive and understand. Indeed, the simplest categories – like male and female – are often the most powerful. In the process of parsing and naming differences and similarities, we create the world – not as a physical thing, but as a thing capable of being known in certain ways and not in others. Language – meaning systems – not only *represents* the world; it *creates* it.

Poststructuralists go further, claiming that the meaning created in a sign is never fixed. It always depends upon the historically particular discourse or text in which it is present, and, following the thought of Jacques Derrida, meaning is produced by differentiating the signifier ('man') from its binary opposite ('woman'). 'Woman' is not present in the text necessarily, but it serves to provide the meaning, through difference, of 'man.' But how do we know what 'woman' signifies? That word itself is defined by reference to another term, that other term defined by yet another. What all this amounts to is the idea that meaning is fashioned not just by means of difference, but by means of constant deferral as well, a continual slipping down a chain of signifiers. Finally, the absent term that defines the signifier 'man' – 'woman' – is the negative of the signifier, and not of equal value to it. It is absent and lesser than the concept it defines.

Now back to Lacan. Just as words gain their meaning through differentiation from their binary opposite, gender identity is formed on the basis of differentiation and distinction. But just as meaning is constantly being deferred in language, the appearance of a coherent, fixed gender identity requires that its opposite be repressed. The bisexual elements existing in Lacan's pre-symbolic child of the unconscious 'imaginary' constantly intrude upon the gendered subject, promising to interrupt the stability, unity, and coherence that he or she presumably enjoys. Repression of these unconscious impulses – the effort to present a coherent gender identity to oneself and to the world – sets up an antagonism between the masculine and feminine elements of the potentially bisexual subject. This battle implies that what we regard as masculine or feminine are no more than constructions we create; moreover, gender identity is constantly under construction, and therefore, presumably, subject to change.

'Change,' that holy grail of the historian's task. But as Scott pointed out, the meanings of gender in Lacan's psychoanalysis are tied to a single signifier, the phallus. And there are but two possibilities for one's relationship to that signifier. In other words, sexual difference seems, once again, to be tied to one universal element. If that's so, Scott lamented, the process of constructing the gendered subject is always the same. No change, after all: that binary opposition of male and female once again appeared eternal.

There was nothing for it, Scott determined, but to insist on the deconstruction of that binary opposition of male/female and the implication of antagonism that accompanied it. Here she turned to Derrida, appropriating his poststructuralist theories of language to call for placing these binaries in their historical context and analyzing how they operated instead of accepting them as the way things were. That analysis would involve reversing the binary opposition to reveal the hidden term that defined the signifier – in our instance 'masculine' – and exposing the hierarchical valuation placed on the two terms. Scott was quick to acknowledge that feminists had been doing something of the same thing for many years now; what was different was her embrace of poststructuralism and postmodernism.

Postmodernism. Isn't that something we should dread? And what is it, anyway? In this section, I hope to explain what postmodernism is, and in doing so, both put to rest the fears critics of it have raised and show how we can use it effectively to do gender history.

Postmodernism refers to a lot of things, because all kinds and varieties of postmodernists exist – in art, architecture, literature, anthropology, politics, philosophy, psychology – you name it, they're there, and they don't necessarily embrace the same ideas.[13] But what all practitioners of postmodernists have in common is a deep skepticism of the belief system by means of which westerners have ordered our thoughts and our practices since the time of the Scientific Revolution and the Enlightenment of the seventeenth and eighteenth centuries. These two momentous movements ushered in the 'modern' against which 'post'modernists position themselves.

The ways of doing things we've inherited from the Enlightenment are so ingrained in us that we don't even think about them – they provide, quite simply, the mental framework within which we walk around in the world. Chief among the principles of the Enlightenment is the conviction that man (and it's important to understand that women were not included under this rubric until the last 50 years or so, as we've seen in the theories laid out in chapter 1, nor were men of color) possesses a stable, coherent self. This Enlightenment self enjoys the capacity to reason – he is rational – and by means of the exercise of his reason, he may know the 'laws of nature' that govern not simply the physical universe but the behavior of human beings in society as well. Through the process of the scientific methods advanced by men like Francis Bacon, René Descartes, and Isaac Newton, he may arrive at truths that hold good for all people and phenomena, that are, in other words, objective and universal. The knowledge accumulated through the uncovering of these truths is self-evidently real; it is out there to be discovered by men using their reasoning faculties; and it can be expressed through a language that faithfully corresponds to the objects being articulated. Because man may know these things in this way, he can free himself from forces that have limited his activities or capacities; that is, he may become an autonomous actor in the world, free. The 'laws of nature' that Enlightenment philosophers appropriated from the scientific revolution to describe how human societies and polities came to be and explain how they work demonstrated to all rational thinkers that history has a purpose. That is, what unfolds over time is not merely the unstructured flow of random events; instead, history develops according to a driving principle which seeks the perfectibility of human beings. Because we can know, we will better ourselves. If we're white, adult men, that is. Finally, the ways of thinking put forth by the Scientific Revolution and the Enlightenment have, ever since, compelled philosophers, scientists, historians, anthropologists, psychologists, and political scientists to search for and produce theories that purport to explain everything succinctly in a grand sweep: a 'unified theory of the "whole,"' as one critic put it.[14]

Postmodernists challenge these fundamental tenets of Enlightenment thought. They see the worldview thrown up by the Enlightenment as a story westerners tell ourselves about the way the world works in order to justify a certain social, political, and economic ordering. They contend that there is no world out there just waiting for us to discover it, just as there is no independent human being who operates freely in and autonomously of that world. Those are fictions. Rather, human beings are always embedded in their surroundings, embedded by language, by history, by our social and economic relations. The knowledge we create cannot be set apart from conditions of life in which we create it: it is a product not of a pure discovery of what exists out there entirely independent of us, but of the kinds of questions we ask, which are themselves a reflection of the conditions of our lives. And because our lives are so different across time, geography, ethnicity, race, class, gender, and culture, there can be no universal truths, only partial ones. Let me say that again: there can be no universal truths. This is not to say that there is no truth;

it is important to follow up that first scary assertion with the second – that there are partial truths. Truths that hold good for certain people or phenomena in certain places at certain times under certain conditions.

Oh, you protest, but what about gravity? That's got to be a universal truth. It was, until Einstein found that it wasn't and put forth his general theory of relativity. Or when quantum mechanics showed that general relativity itself couldn't account for all the forces in the universe. The discoveries of Newton, Einstein, and hundreds of thousands of other scientists, humanists, and social scientists have changed our lives in untold ways, there is no question about that. These specific or partial truths – this knowledge we possess – are wonderful in and of themselves, but somehow they are not enough for us. We persist in trying to bring everything and everybody under a universalizing 'law'; we don't seem to be able to tolerate contradiction, insufficiency, partiality, difference, conflict, ambiguity, or ambivalence. So we come up with these unified field theories as a way to compensate for the anxieties such anomalies create in us; we insist on ordering them in such a way – in linear, binary, hierarchical, holistic, or teleological fashion – as to compel them to fit.

But they don't. Because they can't, given that we are creatures who live not in an abstract world devoid of power, meaning systems, or material inequalities. We live in specific relations of power with one another, in the context of meaning systems – culture – and material systems that are incomplete, messy, and particular.

Postmodernists ask us to acknowledge these specificities; to appreciate that we do not possess a coherent, stable, ever-reliable 'self' that operates above the fray of that messy world; to recognize that the Enlightenment narrative is a fiction that helps us to organize that messy world, from whose ensnarements we can never be sprung, however much we insist otherwise. They ask us to 'deconstruct' these fictions in order to show them for what they are and what they are not.

This is the context within which Joan Scott offered her new theory of gender. She did not accept the position of some postmodernists that the discipline of history was just one more of those fictional narratives that came out of the Enlightenment. But she did argue that we ought to take a good look at the way we practice history and to be upfront about the assumptions we make in doing it. She shared the conviction that the search for a single origin of things – in this case the inequalities between men and women – was not merely futile but misleading. Rather, she insisted, 'we have to conceive of processes so interconnected that they cannot be disentangled.'[15] And we had to understand how those processes worked if we were to understand what they produced. The object of history should no longer be the search for universal, general causation but an explanation of the meanings attached to any variety of activities, events, identities, experiences. Explaining meaning should take place at the level of both the individual and society, and it must incorporate the relationship of one to the other if an understanding of how gender worked and how change took place were to be achieved. Lastly, she urged historians to approach the notion of power in new ways, singling out Michel Foucault's treatment of it as a promising possibility.

Foucault argued that power in modern society (by which he meant the West since the end of the eighteenth century) inheres in a variety of practices and institutions though which the human subject is constituted.[16] He suggested that the human subject was made through a proliferation of practices and institutions and techniques that together constitute what he calls 'discourse.' Discourse is a sophisticated term for something as seemingly simple as conversation, discussion, and communication. It often connotes *serious* speech, writing, or conversation, distinguishing it from the casual speech of everyday language. In particular, Foucault used the term to refer to *technical* speech used by 'experts' in the fields of the social and human sciences – physicians, scientists, prison administrators, educators, psychiatrists, and the like.

But Foucault used the term 'discourse' to mean more than simply speech. It incorporated the *institutions* inhabited by such experts and all the things that they did there. Discourses about crime, madness, or sexuality, for instance, involved the ways prisons, asylums, and hospitals were conceptualized and operated.

For Foucault, discourses enabled the exercise of *power* through the creation and mobilization of expert knowledge. When a medical doctor at an asylum created knowledge, that doctor also created *power*. When a school headmaster figured out ways to gather statistics about the school's students, that headmaster was creating knowledge – and creating a kind of *power* that could be put to work upon the students. Surely, you have experienced such things yourself: automated grading systems, standardized texts, online paper submission systems, and surveillance cameras in the American high school, for example. Scientists, educators, physicians, psychologists, and the institutions within which they worked created knowledge and used it to 'normalize' and thereby police behavior. In doing so, they created and wielded power.

In this sense, power did not emanate from some central location. Indeed, Foucault made his argument by drawing a distinction between the old days, when people thought that power was centralized. It came from God, passed through the figure of the king, and then spread through a hierarchy of officials across the land. The 'new' kind of power that Foucault hoped to explain was not like that at all. It was made over and over again, in small ways, and differently, in every school, prison, hospital, military training ground, and asylum.

Foucault conceived of power not simply as decentralized; he also saw it as diffuse. Power in pre-modern western regimes derived from the king's authority – that is, the authority of the state – to punish by taking human life. Power in the modern world operates at the farthest reaches of society and it does not rely on such a threat as death. Using the metaphor of the human heart and circulatory system,

Foucault described this new power as 'capillary' power, a working of power at the farthest remove from the heart and the center. Capillary power affects people in the living of their everyday lives, in the practices they participate in as they go about the business of living. Moreover, this kind of power operates continuously and in this it is also different from the pre-modern power of the king. The king's power was imposed through an agent of the state, who was usually not around. Rather than being continuous, then, the king's power was occasional and intermittent, exercised when one of his lords or sheriffs dropped by for the annual visit.

This modern power, you will have observed, is both a lot more difficult to grasp and to understand – and a lot more effective than that of the poor king. The king's power was, in essence, a negative force, denying or censoring the expressions, needs, wishes, and desires of people. This new modern kind of power actually *produces* those expressions, needs, wishes, and desires. It is a productive power, in other words, rather than repressive or prohibiting power. Because it operates at so local a level – so diffuse, so decentralized, so omnipresent and everyday – Foucault's power can be thought of as being both broad and intimate. It is as large as the world itself, and as small as a gesture made by a particular individual on a particular second of a particular day. It is everywhere in what he referred to as 'micro-practices'; that is, the social practices that make up peoples' everyday lives. And it is this kind of power – micro, capillary, everyday, working through discourses – that produces you and me as subjects.

Gendered subjects, which brings us back to Joan Scott. She laid out what she meant by gender in two separate but interrelated parts. First, she explained, gender is 'a constitutive element of social relationships based on perceived differences between the sexes.' Secondly, she continued, 'gender is a primary way of signifying relationships of power.' Both these assertions need to be unpacked, which she proceeded to do. The first part of her definition comes down to this: we organize our societies and the relationships we have in them on the basis of what we believe are the differences between men and women and the valuations we place on them. We arrive at those beliefs – we create knowledge about sexual difference – in a number of ways. First, our cultures create and utilize symbols in a variety of often contradictory representations. Scott's example is the prevalence of the Eve/Mary symbol in the Christian West to represent woman. So, is woman Eve or Mary? When, why, how, and in what contexts is she one or the other? That's what historians should ask about the use of this symbolic representation, Scott contended.

Secondly, these symbols carry with them 'norms' for particular kinds of behavior, and those norms are usually articulated through the establishment of binary oppositions that insist upon a single meaning for male and female, masculine and feminine. These norms appear natural and unproblematic in our cultures when, in fact, as poststructuralists would argue, they depend upon the repression or negation of other possibilities. How those other possibilities became obscured, Scott urged, should be the object of historical inquiry. So, in her example, we shouldn't accept uncritically the assumption in a lot of women's or gender history that separate sphere ideology appeared in whole cloth in the late eighteenth and early nineteenth centuries. Rather, we should uncover the contests and conflicts that it aroused as it came into being. In other words, we should not let those apparently fixed gender binaries stand without interrogating them – what was the nature of the debates over separate-sphere ideology? Who engaged in them? Where did they take place?

The third aspect of Scott's definition insisted that as we go about deconstructing those fixed binaries, we must include the political in our sights. We can't simply look at the family or the household to see how gender has worked; we have to broaden our scope to take in such arenas as the labor market, education, and the polity or state. Yes, indeed, the home and family still serve as important areas in which gender relationships are produced, but if we are ever to understand gender in all its depth and breadth, we must give up the outmoded belief that what takes place in kinship systems to construct gender is enough. It's not. What goes on in the economy and in the state has enormous impact on the fashioning of gender.

And finally, we have to come back to the gendered identity of the individual subject. As we've seen, psychoanalysis offers important concepts about how we become gendered subjects, but, Scott observed, 'if gender identity is based only and universally on fear of castration, the point of historical inquiry is denied.'[17] Not only that, but many men and women in real life don't live up to the gendered and sexual norms prescribed for them, or don't always, at any rate. We've got to ask how gender identities are constructed in particular historical contexts – to place the individuals and even larger collectivities within the framework of the social, political, and cultural milieus in which they came up.

The four elements traced above offer a way to see how gender relationships are built, and all of them are necessary to understand that process. The second part of Scott's formulation – that 'gender is a primary way of signifying relationships of power' – lets us watch gender operating in arenas where women themselves are absent. She was quick to admit that gender is not the *only* field on which or through which power is represented and articulated – class and race are obvious others – but in the West at any rate and in the religious traditions of Judaism, Islam, and Christianity it has played a vital role. Concepts about and symbols of gender, regarded as objective, natural, and fixed, structure power; they legitimate differential distributions of power such as material or cultural resources by providing a way to represent those differentials as if they were natural and fixed. Gender becomes an intrinsic part of both the conception and the establishment of power relationships. Gender and power, in other words, if we take the two aspects of Scott's proposition, construct each other. They do so in many different ways, depending upon the historical context in which they are operating.

Back to that *sine qua non* of history, change. How does change take place within this framework of gender and power? In lots of ways. Wars, revolutions, famines, economic depressions, epidemics – all of these may cause such great upheaval in the lives of people and states that the concepts and representations that cultures have used to depict gender have to be altered to make sense under a new order. But it's important to note that gender representations in these instances may not change – they might be rendered even more inflexible in order to legitimate a new regime. Whether they change or not will be determined by a contest over power – over access to material and other resources – and that's what historians should investigate. By bringing gender and power in all its manifestations under their microscopes, to ask questions about how each works to inform and establish the other, Scott contended, historians can't help but transform the discipline of history, as the practitioners of women's history had hoped all along.

4 Theorizing Gender and Power

The impact of Scott's article was immediate and profound. Scott's formulations enabled historians to do more than merely write women into history, an enterprise that had had little success in compelling historians to rethink their conclusions and that seemed to relegate women's history to a separate sphere, to ghettoize it. Conceived in the way Scott formulated it, gender created a lens through which various societies had to be seen anew. Gender could no longer be so easily dismissed as having little effect on traditional historical studies. Scott's theory gave women's and gender history great impetus, provoking an outpouring of works that have transformed the discipline by taking seriously her injunction that identities, categories, and concepts have histories that need examination. It became far more difficult to treat women as if they possessed an essential character, which made treatments of them more nuanced and more true to the reality of women's very complicated lives.

▶ Implications

Masculinity

And, it became clear very shortly, gender necessarily involved men. But not 'men' as they had been treated in historical works since time immemorial; not men as the exemplar of 'humanity,' the standard against which all else was measured. As Gisela Bock noted in 1989, men had escaped the category of gender; they 'could appear to exist beyond gender relations.'[1] A new historical focus on the history of masculinity, undertaken by such historians as Alain Corbin and Robert Nye, required that men and masculinity became problematized.[2] These categories became questions to be answered; their 'construction,' like that of women and femininity, fell under careful scrutiny. As a consequence of these studies masculinity became *visible* as an aspect of men's lives that deserved attention and investigation, enabling historians to offer a more complete, more nuanced, more accurate portrayal of male subjects. No longer two-dimensional creatures who acted, one could imagine, in almost robotic fashion in an entirely public realm, men and their gendered and sexual identities became subject to analyses that revealed the pressures, anxieties, hardships, and exhilarations men at different times and in different places might encounter, in both public and private life.

One of the earliest theoretical treatments of masculinity came out of Australia, where in 1987 sociologist R.W. Connell published *Gender and Power: Society, the Person and Sexual Politics*. As he put it, he was searching for theories that would help him to 'understand a play of social forces in which gender has a major part,' and he offered the concept of 'hegemonic masculinity' as an entity that had to be historicized.[3] Not unlike the concept of patriarchy, hegemonic masculinity required historicization: what forces operated at different moments in different cultures to produce gender imbalances and gender inequalities? How did hegemonic masculinity appear at various places and times? Histories of manliness and masculinity seeking to address questions like these appeared in abundance from all quarters of the world.[4]

Experience and identity

Scott's propositions, if taken to heart, required that gender historians think anew about the object of their study. Women's historians – like all historians – had been concerned with recovering the *experiences* of women (or, in the case of mainstream historians, men) in the past, on the basis of which their subjects discovered a common set of goals or grievances and acted to secure or challenge them. Experience, in fact, had served as one of the most sacrosanct foundations of historical analysis; it gave subjects an *identity*; and it authorized and grounded the agency of historical subjects. Historians need only find out what those experiences and the identities they constituted were, and explain how and why they produced certain behaviors among groups who shared them. Even as feminist historians became more and more skeptical about the possibilities of writing purely objective history, the experiences they wrote about, if conveyed accurately, could be relied upon to tell the truth about the past. The past was out there, in the form of experiences. Our reliability as historians could be measured by the fidelity with which we recounted them. As Louise Newman put it in an important article, 'although history, the *accounts* of experience, may no longer be objective, the underlying experiences still are.'[5]

Scott insisted that the concepts of 'experience' and 'identity' themselves must be historicized. Historians must not assume that experience or identity are entities out there to be discovered by the intrepid scholar. They are, rather, produced by meaning systems in particular cultures at particular times, and it is the job of the historian to uncover the processes by which they are produced. It is important to note that Scott was not saying that people don't experience things or feel themselves to have an identity, or that they don't act on the basis of those experiences and identities. They do, certainly. But those experiences and identities are an *effect* of the discourses – the expert knowledge, the social institutions, the belief systems, the cultural symbols – that construct identity and experience and give them meaning. The processes do not unfold effortlessly but are themselves contested by various groups in society – they are, in other words, political. Scott regarded politics, in fact, as the 'process by which plays of power and knowledge constitute identity and experience.'[6]

The arguments of Denise Riley in *'Am I That Name?' Feminism and the Category of 'Women' in History* provide one way of thinking about how 'experience' and 'identity' operate historically. Riley suggested that the category of 'women' is historically constructed, and is therefore an unstable entity, an erratic collectivity that cannot be relied upon to hold a constant meaning either across cultures or across time. It is always relative to other categories, such as Nature, Class, Reason, and Humanity, which themselves change over time. Just who and what the term 'women' is positioned against is of singular importance to the task of defining and articulating a feminist identity at any historical time and place, for the 'unmet needs and sufferings [of women] ... spring from the ways in which women are positioned, often harshly or stupidly, *as* "women".' Riley saw feminism as the 'site of the systematic fighting-out of that instability' that is 'women.' Although a demarcating of the collectivity that is 'women' is vital to the establishment of a feminist movement, feminists must both concentrate on *and* refuse the identity of 'women.'[7]

Judith Butler expanded upon Riley's rejection of the notions that we possess a coherent, intelligible gender identity. Drawing on the work of Michel Foucault, she saw this Enlightenment bedrock principle as a regulatory practice working on behalf of the exercise of power. Think back to the previous chapter, in which I explained Foucault's belief that power in modern society inheres in a variety of practices and institutions though which the human subject is constituted. Foucault suggested that the human subject was made through a proliferation of practices, institutions, and techniques that together constitute what he called 'discourse.' And it is this kind of power – micro, capillary, everyday, working through discourses – that produces you and me as subjects. But how does it work, exactly, to produce us as subjects? Foucault explained it by means of 'disciplining.'

Discipline and subjectivity

We are 'disciplined' and made 'normal,' Foucault argued,[8] through various techniques, among the most important of which involves surveillance, or the use of the 'gaze' to make visible, control, and manage large numbers of people. The 'gaze' is capable of bringing into view a large population – of prisoners, patients, or students, for instance. It does this through the collecting of massive quantities of information and the assembling of that information in categories that produce knowledge. Think, for example, of the US census. It creates knowledge about large categories of people: who and how many live where? Of what race? Of what income? Of what citizenship? This kind of surveillance *unifies* and organizes a random mass of data.

At the same time, the gaze also *divides* and individualizes. It creates specific, precise, detailed, and intimate information about a specific person. 'Experts' such as physicians or psychiatrists extract from patients the most minute details of their lives, turning people into 'cases' about whom these experts amass a great deal of knowledge. The proliferating records that result *produce* the expertise and power that normatize the individual and make correction possible. So we are simultaneously subjects to both a very specific understanding of *our individual selves* and a universal knowledge that will be used to 'discipline' us, to bring us into a state of 'normal.'

It is not simply the case that these discourses and techniques, institutions, and pieces of knowledge force us into social conformity, discipline us. They do, but it is equally true that we are *made* – and, to some extent, make ourselves – in relation to the broad gaze of a collection of institutions (think of them all: credit-reporting bureaus, banks, phone records, all the data that we give up every time we use the internet). To help think about the ways that surveillance, knowledge, and discourse expand beyond institutions and come to permeate the entirety of social life, Foucault used a concrete example, which he turned into a metaphor for the ways that power and subjectivity work in the modern world. The example was a prison, imagined by Jeremy Bentham (an eighteenth-century social theorist) in 1785, called the 'panopticon,' an architectural device designed to render large numbers of people visible from a single, central viewpoint and then providing organizational plans that categorize them.

Think of inmates of a prison whose cells ring the walls of the building, observable from a tower in the middle of the space. The warden or guard can observe all of the prisoners while remaining virtually invisible to them. Or think of hospital wards organized according to the diseases presented by patients, or a classroom arranged according to the age and/or ability of the students. Think of workers manufacturing goods on a factory floor under the surveillance of managers who can look down upon them from second-floor observation points where their offices are located.

Because the inmates of the prison cannot see into the central tower, they don't know when they are being watched. But the very possibility that their every move is being observed leads them to police *themselves*, to behave in a particular way just in case a guard is looking at them. Workers carry out tedious, repetitive tasks at their mechanized looms or on the assembly line, aware that foremen *could be* watching their every move. Or not. But *that's* the point: we don't know if we're being watched, but we sure do act as if we are. We internalize the gaze, in other words, and perform self-surveillance. No one has to enforce discipline on us, because we enforce it upon ourselves. In this sense, society itself is like one giant panopticon.

Jeremy Bentham's model prison becomes a metaphor, or a way of thinking about, the entire social world as a whole. The product of this entire complex, Foucault said, was the 'disciplining' of populations, a process through which society produces 'docile and useful bodies,' as he put it.

One classic example of Foucault's formulations concerns sexuality. He noted that during the nineteenth century the discussion of sex and sexuality, far from being censored and silenced, actually flourished; that the era witnessed what he described as 'the great process of transforming sex into discourse.' Physicians played a major role in the creation and multiplication of discourses concerning sex; they took it upon themselves to discover and guard 'the truth of sex,' to act as arbiters in formulating sexual norms and the sexual identity of individuals. In the hands of doctors, sexuality became transformed from one element of individual identity to a major determinant of personal identity. So, in the eighteenth century, for example, a man might be a husband, father, American, Bostonian, merchant or craftsman, and lover of men. In the course of the nineteenth century, that multifaceted individual became, in the hands of physicians employing discourses about sexuality, a 'homosexual.'

One component of identity now stood in for the whole person, superseding all other attributes and constituting that individual as 'perverse.' Doctors defined sexuality as particularly susceptible to unhealthy, even pathological developments, and therefore an area that called for their intervention. That intervention – an act of power – was made possible through the production of knowledge. These dynamics were particularly salient for white, middle-class women, whose bodies were, in the hands of physicians, turned into vessels of disease and hysteria, as we've seen in previous chapters. Regarded as 'thoroughly saturated with sex' and inherently pathological, women's bodies became the central object of much medical pronouncement and practice. The constitution of persons as a particular kind of sexual individual and the categorization by experts of that sexuality as normal or abnormal compelled men, women, and children to live in relation to those internalized norms. They policed themselves. They made themselves – and were made – into subjects.

Discourses, in other words, make, classify, and order people in the world, a practice that is inherently political; that is to say, it involves relations of power. And because the operations of power occur at the everyday level of social practices, power is everywhere, inherent in every relationship one involves oneself in. It is *not* simply located in the dominations of the state or of economic institutions. You, dear reader, are on the receiving end of operations of power simply by virtue of your attendance in a class – to say nothing of the myriad other things happening in your life.

But all is not lost. You are not necessarily stuck in a prison-house of language, a discursive system from which there is no escape. For, crucially, discourses that establish the knowledge/power mechanisms in society can also be seized by individuals or groups to resist the operations of power. Foucault called these 'reverse discourses,' or discourses of resistance; he thought of them as ways that people might incorporate the vocabulary and categories of the dominant discourse to assert alternative claims to power.

All of Foucault's theorizing about discourses and power were in service of his overriding project of understanding how human beings came to be constituted as subjects in modern western culture. One came to be a subject through surveillance and domination, knowledge and power. Foucault insisted that we have to see power as not simply dominating, but also as *productive*. It constrained us even as it made us human.

Butler sees the *gendered* subject being produced in precisely this context. How does this happen? Think back to Beauvoir's assertion that 'one is not born a woman, but, rather, becomes one.' She meant that one is forced by society to take on the identity of a woman in ways not dissimilar from those outlined by Foucault. Butler got a little more specific. She turned to psychoanalyst Roy Schafer's contention that we build our identities by identifying with an object – a mother, a father, a sibling. Importantly, that identification takes place not with the *real* person before us but with the person we *fantasize* that object to be: the mother we wish we had, the father we thought we had, the sister or brother we've conjured into a protector. If our identity is fashioned through identification, and if that identification is based on a fantasy, it follows that our identity is a fantasy as well, one that we incorporate and act out in daily life. In other words, said Butler, gender is a performance. It isn't an essence we possess once and for all; we don't have a core of being that is gendered. We *perform* gender in the context of the cultural prohibitions and taboos that surround us, which are themselves a means of exercising power. Gender is a product, in other words, of a particular set of power relations. As Butler put it, 'gender is always a doing, though not a doing by a subject who might be said to preexist the deed.... There is no gender identity behind the expressions of gender; that identity is performatively constituted by the very "expressions" that are said to be its result.'[9]

▶ Imprecations: Scott's critics

Not all feminist historians embraced Scott's, Riley's, and Butler's notions without reservation, to put it mildly. Some cautioned that a focus on gender – especially as it included men within its frame – might divert attention away from women, allowing scholars to leave them out of historical accounts again. Hard-fought struggles to include women as actors in historical world events might be jeopardized. Others objected to the poststructuralist approach that Scott had taken, arguing that examining *representations* of sexual difference left real flesh-and-blood women out of the picture, to their disadvantage as well as the disadvantage of a feminist politics that seemed to rely on a solidarity of women to go forward. If 'women' were mere products of language, critics demanded, how can we explain agency and change? Some believed that a reliance on Foucault's notions of power depoliticized it and obscured the workings of power in the state. And others simply believed that poststructuralist theories were unnecessary – that feminists had all along been doing what Scott urged them to do.

The first objection to the use of 'gender' concerned the possibility that 'women once again will be lost sight of,' as Marilyn Lake explained. 'Gender' seemed far less threatening to men's political or academic enterprises and obscured the feminist challenge offered by women's history and feminism. 'Men do not seem to mind "gender" so much,' noted Lake, 'they have "gender" too. It is women who are beyond the pale.' Lake called for a deconstruction of the 'universal' categories of analysis conventionally used by historians so as to expose their masculine specificity, but she also cautioned that in so doing feminist historians should not lose sight of women as the subject of their inquiries. Analyzing the gendered nature of power and politics, as Scott urged, Lake suggested, 'may only serve to give men's history a new legitimacy and to perpetuate the silence about women.'[10]

This concern flowed from the conviction that gender history required that equal time be devoted to men as to women, masculinity to femininity, as if they were of equivalent significance in any particular study, as June Purvis and Amanda Weatherill put it. Such practices might well lead to gender history being no different than men's history as it had always been written, with the word 'gender' sprinkled liberally throughout but no attention paid to women's lives. Gender history served as a 'male tool' that could be used to 'dissipate women's power whereby women become historically viable subjects only when placed alongside men, thus reinforcing their position as "other."' Gender history 'decentres the study of women as women' by enabling the practice to be incorporated into what she and her co-author called 'malestream' history. And that kind of incorporation, claimed the authors, 'rapes women of the legitimacy to historicize women.'[11]

The choice of the word 'rape' to characterize the implications of gender history for women's historians and the titles of two responses to Scott – the 1993 'If "Woman" Is Just an Empty Category, Then Why Am I Afraid to Walk Alone at Night?' by Laura Lee Downs, and Joan Hoff's 'Gender as a Postmodern Category of Paralysis' (1994) – suggest that her insights were deeply disturbing to and disruptive of more traditional feminist approaches to history.[12] Downs's fear of walking alone at night and Hoff's equation of poststructuralist or 'gender' historians with violent pornographers suggest threats that go beyond the merely intellectual. The allusions to sexual violence betrayed a profound, if vague, sense of personal danger that was displaced, somehow, onto poststructuralism.

Hoff took issue with poststructuralism on three grounds. First, it is antithetical to the assumption of linear chronology and of cause and effect that underlie the historical enterprise. Postmodern theories cannot ever be 'history-friendly,' according to Hoff, because they disavow the empiricism upon which most history has been based since World War II. Postmodernists, she asserted, dispute the existence of a real, material world in which individuals have agency or in which cause and effect can be detected. 'All that can be described using poststructuralist methodology is the moment of observation that has no past, present, or future. Therefore, historical agency – real people having an impact on real events – is both impossible and irrelevant.'[13]

Secondly, poststructualism is misogynist in origin and cannot without great difficulty be adapted to include women. Hoff relied on the work of Somer Bodribb to make this argument, which goes something like this: the misogynist nature of postmodern theories derives from an ideology in which, as Simone de Beauvoir saw it, 'appearances are everything ... [and] the whole real world disappears into thin air.' The connection here between misogyny and postmodernism? 'Based on the massaging of "privileged texts," deconstructionist methodology has been described as an intellectual form of "masturbation,"' explained Hoff, 'that results in an "endless deferral of sense." Thus,' she continued – 'thus?':

> American poststructuralism defers feminism in two primary ways. First it defers radical feminism in the same way that violent pornography objectifies women – it dismembers and disconnects women from any material experiential base. By disconnecting women from their factual context, females are annihilated through disassociation and physical violence, just as radical feminism is destroyed by dispossession from its political roots through the phallologocentric theories of postmodernism.[14]

Thirdly, according to Hoff, postmodernism renders its practitioners, and potentially all feminist activists, politically paralyzed. Here the reasoning is stunningly simple: it does so because its theories 'arose out of a situation that male intellectuals found political[ly] paralyzing in postwar Europe.' The greatest sin of poststructuralists is that they bring about the erasure of women, not just from history, but from virtual existence. With poststructuralism, Hoff argued, the examination of material and cultural representations of biological differences that was gender analysis in the years before Scott's article appeared became transformed into the deconstruction of mere abstract representations of sexual and other differences, with unhappy results:

> Thus, material experiences become abstract representations drawn almost exclusively from textual analysis; persona; identities and all human agency become

> obsolete, and disembodied subjects are constructed by discourses. Flesh-and-blood
> women, of course, also become social constructs, according to poststructuralists,
> with no 'natural' or physiological context except as a set of symbolic meanings
> constructing sexual differences.

Without real, flesh-and-blood women with a common set of experiences out of
which to formulate a set of grievances and act upon them, there can be no feminist
politics, Hoff believed.[15]

In her lamenting of what she saw as the attack on women's history by gender
historians, Hoff laid bare, however inelegantly, one of the most deeply unsettling
elements of postmodernism: its conviction that our identities – we as subjects – are
not stable and coherent but fractured and fluid. The idea that any stable, coherent sense of self we possess is but a fiction is indeed a scary thought, and it is
especially problematic for people and groups who are trying to mobilize themselves in order to redress grievances and demand change. Postmodern thinkers
seek to decenter the subject, as the phrase goes; in the olden days, that subject
was the Enlightenment citizen – white, male, autonomous, and rational. But if
the subject being decentered turns out to be white women, men and women of
color, or gays, lesbians, or transgendered folks who depend upon a sense of common experiences, needs, and desires to form themselves into an interest group in
order to redress their marginalized situations, then this decentering and fragment-
ing can feel undermining, to say the least. Maybe even paralyzing. As Catherine
Hall noted in a review of Riley and Scott's work, it 'can lead to a loss of any notion
of agency.'[16]

These fears derive from the insistence of many on separating out 'language' and
'discourse' from 'the material' or 'the real,' on treating 'language' and 'discourse' as
words or speech. As Christine Stansell put it in her review of Scott's essay, 'On Language, Gender and Working-Class History,' political radicalism found its genesis
'in the realm of a social experience quite distinct from the realm of speech and
text.'[17] When Scott and others like Riley asserted that identity and experience were
the effects of 'discursive' systems, did they mean that women had no materiality, that the body or the psyche could not be said to exist? No, no, and again
no. They meant that the experiences of the body or the psyche and the meanings we imputed to those experiences could not make themselves known outside
of our capacity to represent them. But didn't Derrida declare that 'there is nothing outside of the text?' Yes, he did, but what he meant by 'text' included 'all the
structures called "real," "economic," "historical," socio-institutional, in short: all
possible referents.'[18] As Mary Poovey noted in *Uneven Developments: The Ideological
Work of Gender in Mid-Victorian England*, texts and subjects are produced by material conditions 'in the ever elusive last instance,' even as she insists that the 'last

instance *is* ever elusive' because 'the material and economic relations of production can only make themselves known through representation.' Because material conditions and representations are interdependent, cause and effect do not work necessarily in one direction. But that does not mean there is no such thing as cause and effect, only that it is or can be multidirectional.[19] Sue Morgan put it very succinctly: poststructuralists are not 'anti-realist.' Rather,

> they do not think there is any direct correspondence between the world and human representations of it that could be described as 'true.' This does not mean that feminist historians cannot reconstruct or re-present women's pasts, but that such re-presentations will always be incomplete and imperfect...In order to make sense of the history of women and feminism we must....impose a linguistic shape upon the past that the past itself doesn't have – we must 'trope' and 'emplot' it, to use Hayden White's celebrated verbs. It is not that women have no existence outside language, then, but that that existence has no 'determinable meaning' outside language – a very different emphasis.[20]

Finally, critics of poststructualism deny that we need it at all, that in fact feminists had long been performing the subversive activities that poststructuralist feminists appeared to be claiming for themselves. 'We did not need post-structuralism to develop gender as a category of analysis,' protested Hall, noting that she and Leonore Davidoff had incorporated much of what Scott had called for in her article. Foucault had not originated the insight that power was dispersed; nor did feminists need poststructuralists to tell them that historical writing 'was a male centred form of knowledge.'[21] But as Sue Morgan points out, Scott's enterprise went far beyond what were undoubted critiques of narrative history by feminist historians. She called into question the very *project* of history itself, subjecting it to the kind of interrogation that would expose its profoundly situated practice. History was not a neutral or innocent ground where inquiry about the past and different cultures revealed what was out there to be discovered. In practicing history, in discovering 'experiences' and 'identities' that compelled 'agents' to take action, we were engaging in the construction of those very categories.[22]

▶ Opportunities

As Judith Butler, Denise Riley, Joan Scott, Jane Flax, Mary Poovey, Donna Haraway and others have pointed out, the epistemological project of the Enlightenment (which includes history), that imputes autonomy, unity, and stability to the individual subject, is itself profoundly political. Poovey noted that the binary thinking that constitutes our symbolic order has acted to create a stable category of women that 'could be collectively (although not uniformly) oppressed.' Its deconstruction is a political act, capable of revealing the exclusions – women, people of color, gays and lesbians and transgendered people – that are necessary in the fashioning of the liberal subject, and of exposing the operations of power that maintain systems of dominance. 'If feminism took deconstruction at its word,' Poovey argued, 'we could begin to dismantle the system that assigns to all women a single identity and a marginal place.'[23]

This is not easy for us to do, for we seem to need a single answer or an all-encompassing explanation for the origins of gender identity or of patriarchy and oppression, and in our zeal to find them, we've ignored or denied whole populations of women who are not white, or middle-class, or western. Jane Flax, a philosopher and psychoanalyst, urged us to do otherwise, to accept the fact that because gender is embedded in so great a variety of very complicated and often contradictory social relations, we cannot expect a single theory to do the trick. Rather, she contended, the very complexity of the phenomena before us calls for new and multiple forms of theorizing. It is no weakness or failure, she argued, to embrace a number of theories to explain the incredibly pervasive appearance of gender in all of our practices. She herself drew upon certain aspects of Freudian psychoanalysis (particularly the concept of the unconscious), object-relations theory (its insistence on the interaction of the child with the mother), and postmodern ideas (about the instability of the self), and rejected others because they fail to acknowledge or address critical elements of what she is seeking to know. Freudian, object-relations, and feminist theorists of difference ignore entirely the possibility of rage and aggression in mothers, for example; postmodernists don't really consider gender, and they pay no attention to aspects of human existence – pain, for instance – that may not be articulated through linguistic or meaning systems. But don't throw out the baby with the bathwater, she cautioned, and don't be afraid to use particular parts of contradictory or seemingly incompatible explanations. A proper critical stance for feminists, to Flax's mind, involves tolerating and even celebrating ambivalence, multiplicity, and ambiguity, and if we can incorporate these admittedly difficult aspects in our theorizing, we will be in a far better position to understand and challenge oppression. In a neat turn of phrase, Flax noted, 'If we do our work well, "reality" will appear even more unstable, complex, and disorderly than it does now. In this sense perhaps Freud was right when he declared that women are the enemies of civilization.'[24]

So, what elements of the various theories we've been reading about might we incorporate in our historical work along with the propositions put forward by Scott, and how might they work for us to address issues of change over time? At the level of the individual, it's useful to think of gender identity formation taking place not on the basis of one's possession of or relationship to particular sexual organs, as biological differences don't allow us to consider how change might occur. Short of sexual reassignment surgery, biology won't change much. What if instead of that we combined object-relations theorists' ideas about gender being a consequence of one's relationship to parents and/or caregivers with Butler's notion of gender being performative? This would yield a situation in which change could be generated by alterations in childcare, parenting practices, and socialization, and would incorporate the notion of the unconscious in our thinking. If, as Butler argued, our gender identity derives from our identifications with our parents, siblings, and others around us, and we see those people behaving in ways that defy conventional female and masculine roles, we might well perform a gender identity along lines that defy those conventions as well. Or maybe not, because, remember, Butler saw that identification with the parental figure as a fantasy. But the key point here is that gender is not an essence but an identification, and that what we see as masculinity and femininity or sexuality are merely expressions of the gender performance we are giving at any particular time.

And here is where history comes in. Many critics of postmodernism insist that people like Foucault deny history. But in fact, postmodernism offers us the opportunity – indeed requires us – to be intensely historical. Historians can demonstrate where the 'expressions' of gender Butler speaks of come from; how they change over time; and what they appear in response to. But this isn't enough, because we must, following Scott, Riley, and Butler, talk about power. Specifically, how do we make the leap from the gendered individual to the larger social institutions of power?

Ideologies and interpellations

Foucault was not the only philosopher concerned with this question. His mentor, Louis Althusser, had offered his own formulations about how humans take on subjectivity and the relationship of subjectivity to power.[25] Both Foucault and Althusser saw subjectivity as a twofold process: of acquiring a sense of self as a subject, on the one hand, and of being made a subject to operations of power, on the other. Foucault located the process in discursive practices, but for Althusser, the process involved not discourses and the institutions through which they practiced, but *ideologies*. He defined these as systems of belief within which we move, often unconsciously, and through which we make sense of the world around us, usually without even thinking about them.

Ideologies might be political in nature, they might be economic in nature, they might be social in nature – they are the 'isms' we create to explain how the world works, or should work. Republicanism, liberalism, socialism, capitalism, fascism, feminism – these (and many, many others) are systems of meaning we use to organize our view of the world, to understand our relationships to others in the world, to make claims about our places in the world, to argue for maintaining or altering the world in which we live. As such ideologies help define the ways we think, they become 'real,' in the sense that we act upon them and thus create the actual situations in which we live our lives.

We might think of these things as formal ideologies – highly structured systems of belief – but we need not limit ourselves to the 'isms' in thinking about ideology. In fact, one way to think about an ideology is as the 'common sense' with which we approach daily life. We don't question it. It seems to us to be entirely natural and spontaneous, and, well, it just *is*. But for Althusser, ideology was what called us into being as subjects, as that combination of subjectivity (sense of self) and of subjection (to the state).

So how is ideology different from discourse? Foucault was not particularly interested in ideologies, seeing in *practices* rather than in *belief systems* the most efficacious means of exercising power. His understanding of power was so interested in the diffuse experience of the everyday that he was also not very interested in the big, overarching institutions of the state itself. Althusser reminds us that it is worth paying close attention to the various bureaucracies and apparatuses of the state. The two bodies of theory function somewhat differently, then, although we can see them as being fundamentally interlocked: ideologies (think of the *content* of belief systems) function within discourse (think of concrete practices). And discourse (think of power constituted through human actions) functions within ideology (think of the human *consciousness* created by belief systems). In other words, these two concepts connect to one another, particularly in terms of ways individuals exist as subjects in relation to the social world.

Althusser's fundamental contribution to this body of thought was the idea of 'interpellation,' which is another way of thinking about the connections between individuals and their cultures and societies. The state, Althusser said, actually *speaks* to your subjectivity. It calls out your name in the most intimate way, and you respond. It sends messages to you in your head! Well, okay, it doesn't really. There is no pipeline from the legislative or executive branch of your government that runs directly through your earbuds to your mind, and thence to the depths of your soul. But if you stop and think about it for a minute in light of Foucault's argument about 'discipline,' the state is in your head every single day.

Here's a little thought experiment that might help make this clear. Imagine yourself sitting at a stoplight at a major intersection at 3:00 in the morning. It's obvious to you after five minutes that the light is broken, and yet you – usually – sit there, waiting for it to turn. Why do you do this? Well, because sitting there on your shoulder, like a good angel, is a tiny little police officer, clad in a uniform with a shiny badge and – in the United States, anyway – a gun, telling you that you know the law and should act accordingly. 'Hey, you!' she says, 'You don't actually *know* that the light is broken, and my real-life avatar might be sitting behind that billboard in a patrol car.' When you hear that 'Hey, you!' you are being 'hailed,' as Althusser put it, into a particular kind of subjecthood, one that is obedient to the laws of society and the dictates of the state. That hailing is the essence of 'interpellation.' Even when (as is likely the case at 3:00 in the morning) you listen to the little rationalist devil on your other shoulder and flick that police officer off and proceed through the light, it's too late. You've already had the experience of being interpellated. You are, indeed, a subject. And just because you drove through the light at 3:00 in the morning, you will not do so the next day at noon, for you know that doing so will likely have *power*-ful consequences. You have internalized – and in so doing, reinforced and reproduced – the dominant relations of power in your society. And, as Althusser saw them, these relations have a great deal to do with the state.

If we put Foucault and Althusser together, we might say that subjects are interpellated through discourse; that is, that we are made social subjects through discursive practices. Foucault's discourses are the processes through which Althusser's ideological mechanisms of the state impress upon you how your society is ordered, organized, and managed.

One particularly useful illustration can help demonstrate how this might happen. Think of the social custom, prevalent for centuries, of men opening doors for women. Imagine all the deliberate bodily movements that this custom involves – the man stepping back, sweeping the woman through with an elaborate arm gesture, following along behind. We might think of all this as the 'discourse' of door-opening. In and of itself, this practice doesn't necessarily carry any social meaning (one person opens a door, another person walks through, the first person follows), but if we place the practice, the discourse, within the ideological system of beliefs in which gender inequalities are naturalized – patriarchy – it speaks profoundly of relations of power. For this act of apparent deference of the man to the woman takes place within a structure that subordinates women to men. Those relations of domination and subordination lie at the heart of the 'door-opening' discourse, and create the conditions within which the door-opening takes place. And this discourse serves to obscure the unequal relations of power between men and women, to mystify them, to make them invisible or natural, even as it serves to reinforce and to reproduce those social relations.[26] In this way discourses and ideologies work together, and within one another. They create individual subjectivities in relation to social beliefs. Those beliefs become social realities as human beings live them in the everyday world. And these belief systems carry a kind of weight and direction to them: they are both pictures of the world as 'it is' *and* templates for how the world *ought to be*. And here's the thing: those templates are *not* of an ideal world of human equality and prosperity. They favor certain groups of people over other groups, and they make these inequalities seem right and natural.

Cultural hegemony

We need to go one step further, for power isn't simply embedded in discursive practices or state agencies.[27] Discussions of inequality in the West often take place in the fields of economics, politics, and social science. And discussions of individual lives often take place in psychology and psychiatry. But 'culture' is the place where inequality, social relations, and human subjectivities are understood, formed, justified, explained, and made commonsensical. The realm of cultural meaning is the place where these things are fought over. As yet another philosopher, Antonio Gramsci, asserted, power is present in a variety of cultural, moral, ethical, and intellectual arenas. Gramsci was concerned with how we internalize ideologies that uphold a particular set of social relations – those pertaining, say, to industrial capitalism. He was particularly interested in the question of 'common sense,' the ways that understandings that we neither question nor really pay any attention to become inscribed in our consciousness.

Why do working-class people, for example, accept a system that is antagonistic to their interests? Why, he wondered, do workers not stop to think through the implications of going to work every day to make a product that is sold by the capitalist for far more than he or she paid the worker to make? It's not just that the industrial bourgeoisie, possessing brute economic power, impose their views, interests, and values on the hapless working classes, which have no choice but to accept them. Working people have all kinds of ways of making their own worlds, rich with meanings and often acutely aware of the inequities of the system. Rather, in the exercise of what Gramsci called 'hegemony,' the dominant social group *persuades* subordinate groups of the social and cultural rightness of the ideology by which the dominant group lives. Through this persuasion, dominant groups establish a kind of cultural and moral – as well as political and economic – unity among people possessing wildly disparate interests. Those people might be expected to espouse markedly different, and antagonistic, ideologies. But they do not – or at least they do not let those differences get in the way of their alignment with the dominant group. The dominant social class, by providing concessions to and effecting compromises with subordinate groups, seems to coordinate its interests with those of subordinate groups. They *lead* society, and they do so by appealing to *cultural* logics and by establishing alliances within the realm of cultural meaning.

Gramsci, like Althusser, was writing out of the economic and social theory tradition inaugurated by Karl Marx. Marx and many of the early writers in the tradition placed most of their emphasis on economics. They focused on an economic base for understanding society, and they paid little attention to culture. Culture was simply the consequence of particular forms of economic and social organization. Gramsci rejected that view. Culture, he said, was its own arena, a kind of battlefield of its own. It was hardly disconnected from economic organization or the state, but it was also partially autonomous. In other words, you could imagine an economic struggle between Main Street and Wall Street or High Street and the City taking place at the same time that a struggle taking place in the cultural arena looked very different – say a fight over patriotism, or gays in the military, or the meaning of stardom, or religious belief, or love. Culture, in this sense, was *anything but* a distraction that took people away from the economic or political things that really mattered. Rather, it was a critical part of the entire social system. Gramsci encourages us to view the cultural realm as interconnected with the social, political, and economic worlds, and it's important that we think of this system as highly complex. Consent must be won, not imposed, and everything that seems counterhegemonic and oppositional is at the same time also working, in some way, in the interests of the dominant hegemonic cultural ideologies and discourses through which individuals make sense of the world. In this way, Gramsci helps make concrete sense of Foucault's assertion that power is not simply a case of domination from above, but is rather an almost infinite negotiation that flows through an unimaginably complicated cultural system. In many ways, the root of that system rests within the popular culture that is visible through any number and kind of texts. To create a consensus among many contesting groups, the moment of consent was special and powerful. Gramsci called such instances moments of 'hegemony.'

In a sense, almost every moment in time is a moment of hegemony, in one way or another. There will always be a group that seeks to lead, to persuade (not impose or dominate) all other groups of the rightness of its ideological belief systems. And there will always be groups that oppose that leading group. Gramsci called these groups 'counterhegemonic,' since their ideologies ran counter to that of the leaders or the society as a whole. Importantly, no group – and no individual – is defined consistently by a single ideology or interest. Leading groups seek to find common ground and to persuade others to align their interests – even if it means subordinating other struggles. The result is a complex system of cultural negotiation and tension.

Gramsci encourages us to view the cultural realm as interconnected with the social, political, and economic worlds, and it's important that we think of this system as highly complex. Consent must be won, not imposed, and everything that seems counterhegemonic and oppositional is at the same time also working, in some way, in the interests of the dominant hegemonic cultural ideologies and discourses through which individuals make sense of the world. In this way, Gramsci helps make concrete sense of Foucault's assertion that power is not simply a case of domination from above but is rather an almost infinite negotiation that flows through an unimaginably complicated cultural system. In many ways, the root of that system rests within the popular culture that is visible through any number and kind of texts.

Gender and race: an example of counterhegemony

The American 1960s provide a good example. Coming out of the 1950s, the United States might have been described – in the terms of cultural hegemony – as a culture of progress, scientific expertise, and state–corporate power. A dominant group consolidated cultural meanings around themes of prosperity, consumerism, and technical prowess. Under this umbrella, however, was a roiling sea of counterhegemonic currents. The African American civil rights movement was developing the tools it would use to attempt to establish itself as a leading cultural movement, trying to establish segregation as abnormal and equal rights as a commonsense good around which most Americans could find consensus. As the Vietnam War heated up, a counterhegemonic movement formed in opposition, and it too developed modes and means of persuasion that it hoped would convince others to follow an antiwar lead. Counterculture groups, disenchanted with the cultural logics of conformity, began offering new systems of belief that emphasized freedom and communitarianism. They, too, sought to persuade others to follow their leadership. Any one of these movements – and of course there were many others – might have won the day, persuading a range of other groups to throw in their lot with a hegemonic consensus.

Women were active in all these movements, and many of them found that their contributions did not receive the respect they deserved. Building on a long history of feminist thought, a new counterhegemonic movement – the women's liberation movement – emerged in the late 1960s and early 1970s. Many women subordinated their feminist interests to what they perceived as the greater cause of civil rights or antiwar movements. Such women would have been making a consensual deal within the framework of hegemony and counterhegemony. They perceived their strongest interests, not in feminism, but in other movements, and were thus willing to join a social group that did not always honor their interests. They gave their consent, in a manner of speaking, to their domination as women. What was counterhegemonic, then (say, the antiwar movement), was at the same time hegemonic (it was patriarchal and made the subordination of women part of its commonsense view of the world).

Some of these movements (civil rights and antiwar movements, for example) achieved at least some of their goals. As they did, women active in these movements changed their cultural alignments, creating new counterhegemonic groups based on feminism. Many of those groups were formed primarily among white, middle-class women and the cultural logic of their feminism represented *those* particular interests. In other words, if the women's movement of the 1970s was counterhegemonic (in that it challenged patriarchy and gender inequality) it was also, along other social lines, hegemonic. Those other lines included race (very few women of color in this new feminism) and class (not so many poor women either). Unhappy with both civil rights and feminist movements, women of color began to form their own organizations to gain liberation for themselves.

This counterhegemonic challenge to white, middle-class feminism from women who were neither white nor middle-class compelled feminist academics to examine a number of assumptions from which they operated as both political activists and scholars. Clearly, one of the fundamentals of western feminist thinking – that women, as both subject and object of feminism's program, share common natures, common needs, common wants, common desires, and a common oppression – could no longer be held so determinedly. Women of color had made it clear that differences in race, sexuality, class, nationality, culture, religion, age, and ethnicity must undermine any such notions of an essential femininity or womanliness upon which feminism might rest. Feminist theorists turned to a variety of traditions to try to deal with what threatened to deliver a knockout blow to feminist politics, for how could a movement seeking to improve the lives of women do so if a unitary category of 'women' didn't really exist? In short, when women of color began to subject the unitary white middle-class woman thrown up by the white middle-class feminist movement to scrutiny and criticism, feminist scholars sought alternative ways of thinking about identity, subjectivity, culture, and power.

Women like Hazel Carby, Valerie Amos and Pratibha Parmar, Elizabeth Spelman, Mrinilini Sinha, Michele Mitchell, Chandra Mohanty, bell hooks, Evelyn Brooks Higginbotham, Himani Bannerji, Elsa Barkley Brown, and Antoinette Burton – and many, many others – compelled historians persuaded by Scott's theory to rethink their approach to gender, to embrace the postmodern call in order to see the ethnocentric and imperialist traditions that informed so much western scholarship. They insisted that gender might *not* be the dominant element in the oppression of women; they urged that race and class not only had to be taken in account in any gender analysis, but, more radically and transformatively, that race and class actually operated to *constitute* gender.

Australian feminist historians had incorporated race in their histories of women and gender pretty early on. In 1975, Anne Summers had published a book entitled *Damned Whores and God's Police*, which she subtitled *The Colonisation of Women in Australia*. She meant white women oppressed by white Australian men, and did not include aboriginal women in her analysis. Criticisms of her usage of the term 'colonisation' soon appeared: one reviewer wondered 'how the potential for rape can be adequately correlated to the situation of the colonised Aborigines who were subjected to the violent dispossession of their lands, murder, rape, mutilation, ravaging diseases and starvation.' Later editions of the book dropped the subtitle.[28] Aboriginal women had already begun to point out the racial blindness of Australian feminism: Pat O'Shane had asked 'Is There Any Relevance in the Women's Movement for Aboriginal Women?' in 1976, and white feminist historians began to reconceptualize their projects in light of her and others' critiques. Ann Curthoys published 'Identity Crises: Colonialism, Nation and Gender in Australian History' in 1993, followed by a spate of other articles and book chapters. One of the most ambitious early approaches came in 1994, with the publication by Patricia Grimshaw, Ann McGrath, Marian Quartly, and Marilyn Lake's *Creating a Nation*. This book sought to tell a feminist version of the creation of Australia as a nation, and it placed the dispossession, displacement, and destruction of aboriginal peoples and their cultures at the center of the story.[29] Subsequent histories of Australia, and they are numerous, have not omitted the questions of race and colonialism from their treatments of women and gender. More importantly, works such as aborginal Australian Aileen Moreton-Robinson's 'Troubling Business: Difference and Whiteness within Feminism' and *Talkin' Up to the White Women: Indigenous Women and Feminism*, both published in 2000, have compelled historians to regard race as including whiteness. Feminism and feminist history has never been the same since.[30]

African American historians have carried out what Darlene Clark Hine called 'a quiet intellectual transformation' in feminist history with their scholarship on black women. Treatments of their lives under slavery, in the context of religious and family life, in labor organizations and philanthropic associations; analyses of black masculinity; and examinations of conflicts and tensions between black men and women in African American nationalist ideologies have dramatically changed our understandings of how gendered and racialized identities have formed.[31] bell hooks, while leery of some of the shortcomings of postmodernism, nevertheless embraces what it has to offer in 'opening up our understanding of African-American experience,' particularly its possibilities of 'reformulating outmoded notions of identity.' It enables historians to look at class and color differences among African Americans, to examine the multiplicity of identities taken on by blacks, and how representations of blackness work to uphold racist and colonial regimes.[32]

From my vantage point as a British historian, some of the most productive uses of gender and race have appeared in postcolonial studies of empire. Works of imperial history, until relatively recently, focused almost exclusively on the economic or geopolitical causes of empire-getting and empire-building, military conquest, or diplomatic maneuvering in the process of obtaining colonies. Postcolonial historians are much more interested in the cultural aspects of imperialism for metropolitan subjects, on the one hand, and the effects of imperialism on colonized subjects, on the other. But perhaps most importantly, postcolonial feminist historians ask about the interrelation of colonizer and colonized, seen especially in the process of constructing identities and subjectivities both in the metropole and in the colony as a product of difference. As Ann Stoler and Fred Cooper put it, 'a grammar of difference was continually and vigilantly crafted as people in colonies refashioned and contested European claims to superiority.' Gender and sexuality provided the ground for a good deal of that grammar of difference. There is so much great work out there – check out the endnotes for a list of just a few among many.[33]

Part III
Doing It

5 Writing Gender History: War and Feminism in Britain, 1914–1930

You've spent a lot of time reading about a variety of theories about gender. This chapter seeks to show how gender as Scott defined it can be used in practice. It focuses on feminism in the interwar period, and offers a counter to history that regards 'experience' as a foundation of human agency. One such example would be Brian Harrison's *Prudent Revolutionaries: Portraits of British Feminists between the Wars*. Harrison included Margaret Bondfield and Susan Lawrence in his study, despite the fact that they did not, he conceded, 'see the world in feminist terms.' Their presence in the book derived from the fact that they sat in parliament. 'What does feminism owe to these parliamentary careers?' Harrison asked. 'Merely by getting into parliament and by operating efficiently there, whatever their views, these…Labour MPs helped to raise society's respect for women.' Virtually any women involved in any politics, if we follow this thinking, qualify as feminists.[1] It won't do.

Harrison's approach exemplifies the limitations of histories that essentialize women, that rely on a direct connection between experience and identity on the one hand and action, or agency, on the other. As Scott observed, 'the lived experience of women is seen as leading directly to resistance to oppression, that is, to feminism. Indeed, the possibility of politics is said to rest on, to follow from, a pre-existing women's experience.' If, as Scott suggested, we shift our efforts away from 'the reproduction and transmission of knowledge said to be arrived at through experience' to 'the analysis of the production of that knowledge' about such categories as gender, class, race, or sexuality – that is, about identity – we can avoid reifying or naturalizing these categories and historicize them.[2] Such an analysis depends on discarding the liberal notion of the autonomous subject who exists outside of or prior to language, and of accepting the idea that experience is constructed discursively.

89

▶ Prewar and postwar feminism

In the case of Victorian and Edwardian feminists, for instance, it was not their experiences that automatically produced their feminism, but their recognition of their subject-positioning in an asymmetrical arrangement created by the ideologies, discourses, and social practices of the nineteenth century. Prewar feminists vigorously attacked the notion of separate spheres and the medical and scientific discourses about gender and sexuality upon which those spheres rested; their feminism lies precisely in their refusal of the sexual discourses that defined gender, in their transgression of the boundaries and practices that upheld the ideological system of sexual difference upon which Victorian and Edwardian bourgeois society rested.

Many feminists after World War I, by contrast, pursued a program that championed rather than challenged the prevailing ideas about masculinity and femininity that appeared in the literature of psychoanalysis and sexology. In embracing radically new – and seemingly liberating – views of women as human beings with sexual identities, many feminists within the mainstream and middle-class National Union of Societies for Equal Citizenship (NUSEC) accepted theories of sexual difference that helped to advance notions of separate spheres for men and women. This shift did not take place suddenly, and was resisted throughout the 1920s by many other feminists, also middle- and even upper-class, who took themselves off to form such organizations as the Six Point Group and the Open Door Council, but the acceptance of the dominant discourse on sexuality represented a fundamental abandonment of prewar feminist ideology. By the end of the 1920s, 'new' feminists found themselves in a conceptual bind that trapped women in 'traditional' domestic and maternal roles, and limited their ability to advocate equality and justice for women.

This chapter, then, demonstrates how change within regimes of gender might take place, seeing in the Great War a prime motive force in transforming certain aspects of gender ideology. The experiences of the Great War – articulated and represented in specific languages of gender and sexuality – forged dramatically different ideas about gender and sexual identity for many men and women from those prevailing in the late Victorian and Edwardian eras; these languages and the identities they spawned provide the context within which interwar feminism operated and by which it was constrained.

The arguments of Denise Riley provide an important starting point for my analysis of interwar feminism. As we've seen, Riley suggested that the category of 'women' is historically constructed, and is therefore an unstable entity, an erratic collectivity that cannot be relied upon to hold a constant meaning either synchronically or diachronically. It is always relative to other categories; just who and what the term 'women' is positioned against is of singular importance to the task of defining and articulating a feminism at any historical time and place. The activities and ideas we as historians identify as feminist at any given time are contingent on the discourses that construct 'women' and on the discourses of resistance that feminists produced in their challenge to society. We must pay attention to the languages feminists utilized and incorporated in the advocacy of their positions. If we fail to examine feminism in the context of the discursive practices that create the gender system out of which it emerged, then the word can have no real meaning for us or for contemporaries.

The outbreak of war in August 1914 brought to a halt the activities of both militant and constitutional suffragists in their efforts to gain votes for women. By that time, the suffrage campaign had attained the size and status of a mass movement, commanding the time, energies, and resources of thousands of men and women, and riveting the attention of the British public. In early 1918, in what it defined as a gesture of recognition for women's contribution to the war effort, parliament granted the vote to women over the age of 30. This measure, while welcome to feminists as a symbol of the fall of the sex barrier, failed to enfranchise some three million out of eleven million adult women. When war ended, feminists continued to agitate for votes for women on the same terms as they had been granted to men; but organized feminism, despite the fact that a considerable portion of the potential female electorate remained disenfranchised, never regained its prewar status as a mass movement. By the end of the 1920s, feminism as a distinct political and social movement had become insignificant. Feminists' understandings of masculinity and femininity – of gender and sexual identity – became transformed during the war and in the postwar period, until they were virtually indistinguishable from those of anti-feminists.

This fundamental change, this embracing of what amounted to an anti-feminist understanding of masculinity and femininity, came about as a consequence of the languages by means of which women's experiences and perceptions of the Great War were articulated. Those women who were able to hold on to prewar understandings about gender – who came to be called egalitarian or 'old' feminists, though many were not old enough to have participated in the prewar suffrage campaign – were those who had experienced the war directly, at the front. Most 'new' feminists, by contrast, saw the war from afar, from home. This difference of position vis-à-vis the war and its participants became manifested in differing sexualized languages by means of which the war was articulated, and accounts, at least in part, for old and new feminists holding fundamentally different understandings about masculinity, femininity, and as a consequence, feminism.

▶ Representations of Sex and War, 1914–1916

The sexual imagery utilized to represent the war changed over time, reflecting developments in the prosecution and fortunes of the war and the extent to which the home front was involved. During the first phase, lasting from August 1914 into 1915, the war was often depicted as a remasculinization of English culture, perceived to have become degenerate and effeminate in the years before August 1914. This kind of representation relied upon a corresponding imagery of women as refemininized, especially in the aftermath of a widespread feminist movement that had challenged the dominant cultural norms of masculinity and femininity. Thus, an assertion of and emphasis on traditional notions of separate spheres for men and women characterized the first year of the war. It was accompanied by the notion of war as unleashed sexual desire, best exemplified by the gruesome tales of German atrocities committed against Belgian women that spread through the land.

The reassertion of separate spheres, with its implied dichotomies of private and public, of different natures of women and men, of home and front, appeared very early, even among feminists. Merely cursory readings of *Common Cause*, the organ of the National Union of Women's Suffrage Societies, reveal a shift of focus from public, political affairs in July 1914 to more traditional women's concerns in August 1914. The National Union itself, in an unreflexive, almost knee-jerk reaction to war, turned to work that emphasized gender divisions, and declared its conviction that feminists' greatest and most obvious responsibilities in sustaining the vital strength of the nation were those pertaining to domesticity. 'We … very early arrived at the conclusion,' Millicent Fawcett, longtime president of the National Union of Suffrage Societies, recalled after the war, 'that the care of infant life, saving the children, and protecting their welfare was as true a service to the country as that which men were rendering by going into the armies to serve in the field.' Indeed, it was the very corollary to men's service. 'While the necessary, inevitable work of men as combatants is to spread death, destruction, red ruin, desolation and sorrow untold,' she told a Kingsway Hall audience in October 1914, 'the work of women is the exact opposite. It is … to help, to assuage, to preserve, to build up the desolate home, to bind up the broken lives, to serve the State by saving life rather than destroying it.' *Common Cause* regularly carried notices on the 'Care of Maternity in Time of War,' and articles and appeals for donations 'To Save the Babies.' The traditional cultural associations of men with war and death on the one hand, and women with home and the giving and preserving of life on the other, emerged with virtually no resistance from feminists; indeed, they were often fostered by feminist rhetoric. As S. Bulan put it in *The Englishwoman*, 'at the call of war, the first thought of every man is to fight, of every woman to nurse.'[3]

'Mothering Our Soldiers' was urged upon readers of *Common Cause*. In September 1914, it suggested that women set up laundry and mending stations in every district where Territorials were camped. In November 1914, Dr. Helen Wilson proposed and *Common Cause* endorsed, in what constituted a literal construction of the home front, the formation of a Women's Army to train in and teach the arts of homemaking.

> The most precious national service that women can render, whether in peace or war, is the care of the home, the guardianship of the family. On this point Suffragists and Anti-suffragists are agreed. Cannot our young women be induced to 'enlist' for this national service[?] Can they not be shown that the most practical service they can render to the absent brother, or husband, or sweetheart, is to ensure him a more perfect home when he comes back to it? This means training.

The Women's Army she envisaged would be organized along the lines of the Territorial Force.[4]

The reassertion of traditional norms of masculinity and femininity and of separate spheres for men and women found expression in the efforts to legitimate and justify the war itself. Much of the official propaganda presented the war as a fight for and on behalf of Belgium, which was usually depicted in the guise of womanhood. 'Little Belgium' evoked images of an innocent woman in need of protection from a paternal male. Such chivalric imagery became charged by and infused with sexual implications, as accounts of the invasion of Belgium and rumors of German atrocities reached England and seared the collective British memory. Much of the atrocity propaganda that circulated throughout Britain focused on outrages committed against women. In May 1915, the government issued the Bryce Report, the findings of a commission charged with investigating stories of German atrocities in Belgium. For one penny, the cost of a daily newspaper, Britons could purchase the 'summary of evidence' and an appendix of selected case histories. In what can only be described as a kind of pornographic orgy that fostered voyeurism and made war sexually 'exciting,' the report told of the following: A Belgian soldier marching along outside Liège came upon

> a woman, apparently of middle age, perhaps 28 to 30 years old, stark naked, tied to a tree. At her feet were two little children about three or four years old. All three were dead. I believe the woman had one of her breasts cut off, but I cannot be sure of this. Her whole bosom was covered with blood and her body was covered with blood and black marks. Both children had been killed by what appeared to be bayonet wounds. The woman's clothes were lying on the grass thrown all about the place.

Another soldier watched Germans

> going into the houses in the Place and bringing out the women and girls. About 20 were brought out.... Each of them was held by the arms. They tried to get away. There were made to lie on tables which had been brought into the square. About 15 of them were then violated. Each of them was violated by about 12 soldiers.... The ravishing went on for about 1½ hours. I watched the whole time.

A soldier retreating 'saw a woman lying on her back inside a house; her skirt was pulled up over her head. There were no clothes on the lower part of the body. She had a wound extending from between her legs (private parts) to her breast.' A Belgian officer testified that 'a young girl of about 17 came up to me crying in the village; she was dressed only in a chemise: she told me that 17 girls including herself, had been dragged into a field and stripped quite naked and violated, and that twelve of them had been killed by being ripped up across the stomach with a bayonet.' A soldier recounted coming across a girl of 14 at Weerde: 'she was half mad when we found her. Her mother was there, and told us that seven Germans had violated her one after another.'[5] A litany of atrocities committed against women and children and civilian men by German soldiers continued for some 238 pages.

This kind of imagery linked sex and war in the conscious and unconscious minds of Britons. The Bryce Report 'released into English imaginations a style, a language, and an imagery of violence and cruelty that would in time permeate imagined versions of the war, and become part of the record,' as Samuel Hynes has noted.[6] It needs to be emphasized that the images of violence and cruelty were images, primarily, of acts against women, so that the rape and sexual mutilation of women served as one of the major means by which the war was imagined and represented by contemporaries.

While the imagery of sexual violation of women served as a means of recruitment and justification for the war, it may well have acted, unconsciously at least, to reinforce the promises of sexual reward and release for enlisting that bombarded the British public. In one song that carried unmistakable undertones of prostitution, long the acknowledged avenue by which British men were first initiated into sexual activity, and by means of which they were expected to find relief from pent-up sexual tension, women urged men to 'take the King's shilling' – to enlist – with the following:

> On Sunday I walk out with a soldier,
> On Monday I'm taken by a tar,
> On Tuesday I'm out
> With a baby Boy Scout,
> On Wednesday with a Hussar.
> On Thursday I gang oot with a Kiltie,
> On Friday the captain of the crew,
> But on Saturday I'm willing, if only you'll take a shilling,
> To make a man [out] of any... of you.[7]

Feminists colluded in representing war as a form of unrepressed sexual desire. Much of the news carried by *Common Cause* dealt not with the war effort – casualty

lists, battles, or troop movements, for example – but with instances of sexual mis-
conduct on the part of (usually working-class) women. In what it decried as 'a
national shame,' the paper carried a plea 'for the protection of our young soldiers, many of them only nineteen, from the solicitations of women.' In October,
Common Cause declared that the large numbers of women hanging around the
training camps, behaving badly and creating 'a real scandal,' had become 'a danger
to themselves and others.' In November 1914, an entire meeting at the Guildhall
was devoted to addressing the problem of women drinking and loitering at the
camps,[8] another indication of the near-obsession with the display of overt sexuality
preoccupying feminists and the general public.

These representations of the sexual imperatives of war were put forward within a
framework of traditional gender and sexual relations, and did not seriously threaten
the bourgeois domestic ideology of separate spheres based upon belief in a single
model of (insistent) sexuality for men and in the dual nature of female sexuality –
that of purity and passionlessness ascribed to middle-class women and promiscuity
and prostitution to working-class women. Images of sexual release, of loosening
the sexual restraints between men and women in the depictions of khaki fever
and stories of war babies, while containing hints of middle-class women adopting
male sexual values and ignoring traditional standards of reticence and chastity,
were nevertheless heavily weighted by class, and could thus adequately represent a war that was still thought about and presented in traditional terms. But
by mid-1915 or so, as those on the home front began to understand that theirs
was not a traditional war, this kind of sexual representation began to change
as well.

▶ Representations of Sex and War, 1916–1918

By 1916, boundaries between home and front could no longer be drawn with ease.
Even before the monstrous casualties of the Somme battles forced Britons to face
up to the realities of war in the twentieth century, the war experience on the home
front was changing dramatically. Britons had to face the fact that this war involved
everyone, not just the men who joined the ranks of the armed forces. A blurring
of identities – of the distinctions between warriors and civilians, between men and
women – was taking place, necessitating a different kind of sexual imagery to represent the war. Thus, in the second phase of war, from about late 1915 on, the
representation of war as unleashed sexual desire gave way to visions of sexual disorder, a blurring of gender lines as women went off to factories and the front to
do war work and men found themselves immobilized in trenches. Toward the end
of the war, sexual disorder came to be depicted as sexual conflict and polariza-
tion between the sexes, or sex war. Sexual conflict finally provided one of the few

adequate means by which the political, economic, and social upheaval occasioned by the Great War could be represented.[9]

As men went off to war, women joined the workforce in unprecedented numbers, taking jobs as munitions workers, agricultural laborers, tram conductors, ambulance drivers, frontline nurses, and, finally, after the disasters of 1916, auxiliary soldiers. The exigencies of the war after mid-1915 dramatically upset the perceived gender system of the Victorian and Edwardian periods. Nina Boyle of the Women's Freedom League could rejoice that 'woman's place, by universal consensus of opinion, is no longer the Home. It is the battlefield, the farm, the factory, the shop.' The dismantling of barriers between men's and women's work fostered a blurring of distinctions that had helped to form gender identity. Rebecca West described her visit to a cordite factory in 1916 in terms that confounded the divisions of home and front. 'It is of such vital importance to the State,' she observed in 'Hands That War,' 'that it is ringed with barbed-wire entanglements and patrolled by sentries, and its products must have sent tens of thousands of our enemies to their death. And it is inhabited chiefly by pretty young girls clad in Red-Riding-Hood fancy dress of khaki and scarlet.' Slipping from war imagery to domestic imagery without drawing attention to any sense of incongruence, West highlighted the dramatic changes wrought by the war. 'When one is made to put on rubber overshoes before entering a hut it might be the precaution of a pernickety housewife concerned about her floors, although actually it is to prevent the grit on one's outdoor shoes igniting a stray scrap of cordite and sending oneself and the hut up to the skies in a column of flame.' The hard work, the long hours, the danger, and, indeed, the deaths of women resulting from munitions explosions, led West to declare that 'surely, never before in modern history can women have lived a life so completely parallel to that of the regular Army.' Mrs. Alec-Tweedie rejoiced in the fact that by the events of the war, 'women have become soldiers.' Moreover, she predicted, it might not be long before 'we may have to have women fighters too.... For...the war has literally metamorphosed everything and everybody. To-day every man is a soldier, and every woman is a man.' She argued for the formation of a Woman's Battalion, foreseeing the day when 'rather than let the Old Country go under, the women of the Empire would be...more than willing, to take a place in the firing line.'[10] This is a far cry from knitting socks and rolling bandages or providing relief for Belgian refugees; the language of traditional femininity, of separate spheres for women and men could not adequately articulate the experiences and requirements of a war that failed to respect the boundaries between home and front, between civilian and soldier.

The association of sex and war carried potentially explosive implications for society when it became clear that this war would require the participation of all segments of the population; anxiety about the prosecution of the war frequently took shape as anxiety about sex, or was articulated in sexual terms. The charges of khaki fever and war babies that predominated in 1914 had contained a kind of patronizing and even good-hearted tone; as the war effort worsened, however, attacks on women's sexuality increased in virulence. Making no distinction between prostitutes on the one hand, and young women infected with khaki fever on the other, Arthur Conan Doyle wrote to *The Times* in February 1917 complaining about 'vile women... who prey upon and poison our soldiers... these harpies carry off the lonely soldiers to their rooms... and finally inoculate them... with one of those diseases.' In July 1918, delegates to an Imperial War Conference heard tales of infected women 'lying in wait for clean young men who came to give their lives for their country.' The Government, for its part, introduced regulation 40d of the Defense of the Realm Act in March 1918, at the height of worries about the German advance, declaring that 'no woman suffering from venereal disease shall have sexual intercourse with any member of His Majesty's Forces.' Clearly, in the minds of many, sex presented as great a threat to the survival and existence of Britain as did Germany; the two were, indeed, often conflated. Mrs. Alec-Tweedie made this connection abundantly clear when she warned that 'every woman who lets herself "go" is as bad as a German spy, and a traitor, not only to her sex, but to her country.'[11]

▶ Sex War

By focusing on sex as one of the major issues of the war, contemporaries hit upon a means by which they could imagine, represent, and even narrate – that is, to make sense of – the war, which defied traditional terms and habits of thought. As women began to take up jobs previously held exclusively by men, and even to serve as auxiliaries in the armed forces, sexual representation utilizing traditional heterosexual terms and images was no longer adequate to the task of giving meaning to a war so completely out of line with all precedent. Visions of sexuality in which middle-class women had become fully as unrestrained as men, and/or that exposed sex as a drive toward violence, war, and death, began to predominate. For instance, although she understood the 'bacchantic frenzy' that struck 'hundreds of reputable women and girls round every camp,' to be 'the natural complement to the male frenzy of killing,' drawing an analogy between sex and death that anticipated Freud, Helena Swanwick 'never learnt to tolerate this with an indifferent mind.' It 'revolted me almost as much as [the war's] more obvious brutalities,' she recalled, in a remarkably bald illustration of the confusion of war and sex. In D.H. Lawrence's 'Tickets, Please,' women tram conductors, 'fearless young hussies,' set upon their inspector, John Thomas, whose amorous adventures with a number of women have infuriated them. Their assault is depicted in near-sexual terms, invoking the imagery of rape and castration.

Their blood was thoroughly up. He was their sport now. They were going to have their own back, out of him.... His tunic was simply torn off his back, his shirt-sleeves were torn away, his arms were naked.... Their faces were flushed, their hair wild, their eyes were all glittering strangely. He lay at last quite still, with face averted, as an animal lies when it is defeated and at the mercy of the captor.

'You ought to be *killed*,' the ringleader told John Thomas with 'a terrifying lust in her voice.' The prospect of women waging war against men was raised by H.G. Wells's *Mr. Britling Sees It Through* in the character of Letty, whose husband Teddy has been wounded and is missing in action. She proposes to form 'The Women's Association for the Extirpation of the whole breed of War Lords,' a band of women dedicated to ending all wars means of 'killing the kind of people who make them. Rooting them out. By a campaign of pursuit and assassination that will go on for years and years after the war itself is over.'[12]

For feminists, too, the connection between sex and war could easily give way to notions of sex war. In April 1915, Emmeline Pankhurst gave a speech infused with the imagery of sexual assault. 'The men of Belgium, the men of France, the men of Serbia,' she lamented to her Liverpool audience,

> however willing they were to protect women from the things that are most horri-ble – and more horrible to women than death itself – [they] have not been able to do it. It is only by an accident, or a series of accidents, for which no man has the right to take credit that British women on British soil are not now enduring the horrors endured by the women of France, the women of Belgium, and the women of Serbia.

Mary Lowndes wrote in *The Englishwoman* in October 1914 that the belief that men protect women had been proved false by the events on the continent. 'And, indeed,' she added, 'we must remember that it is against themselves, against animal dominance and brute force, that men must learn to protect their women in days of peace, if there is to be any hope that in time of war they shall have the same immunity that (at any rate theoretically) is extended to peaceable non-combatants of the other sex.' Nina Boyle reported to readers of *The Vote*, the official newspaper of the Women's Freedom League, in February 1915 that 'British officers and officials are treating as gentlemen and soldiers, and not as criminals, men guilty of the foulest horrors'; she wrote 'of a train full of school-girls...who were outraged by officers,' and cited a statement in the medical journal, the *Lancet*, 'that of a convent of sixty nuns, twenty-nine are expecting to be confined [by pregnancy] as the result of similar brutal treatment.' The line between German soldier and British soldier was not very distinct in the rhetoric of these women, and Boyle very soon erased it entirely. 'Greatest of all dangers to women,' she wrote in August 1915, 'is the unbridled passion of men...even now, in war time, in our own land, from our own men, the danger stalks undiminished and unchecked.'[13]

The picture of masculinity conjured up by such imagery was often that of 'mechanical dolls who grin and kill and grin,' 'a grimacing phantom,' 'a creature at once ridiculous and disgusting,' as R.H. Tawney described it resentfully in October 1916 while recuperating from wounds received on the Somme in July. He castigated the newspapers for 'inventing a kind of conventional soldier' who revels in the 'excitement' of war and finds ' "sport' in killing other men,' and hunts 'Germans out of dug-outs as a terrier hunts rats.' 'We are depicted as merry assassins, rejoicing in the opportunity of a "scrap" in which we know that more than three-quarters of our friends will be maimed or killed, careless of our own lives, exulting in the duty of turning human beings into lumps of disfigured clay.' 'The Happy Warrior' depicted by Herbert Read in 1916 in a poem dripping with contempt for those at home who continued to think of the war in chivalric terms, whose 'aching jaws grip a hot parched tongue,' and whose 'wide eyes search unconsciously,' gave read-ers a picture of a mute automaton dribbling bloody saliva down his shirtfront as he stabbed and stabbed again 'a well-killed Boche.' Moreover, the imagery of sex-ual assault raised by the Belgian atrocities continued to inform representations of the war. Valentine Wallop, in Ford Madox Ford's *Parade's End*, believed that 'all manly men were lust-filled devils, desiring nothing better than to stride over bat-tlefields, stabbing the wounded with long daggers in frenzies of sadism.'[14] Such representations of masculinity bore little resemblance to the way men at the front perceived themselves or women at the front perceived them, but the power of these bloodthirsty images was lasting, and would have significant impact on the way middle-class women at home understood the nature of masculinity, femininity, and the relations between the sexes.

Feminists who spent some part of the war in arenas in which the war was actu-ally prosecuted or where the direct consequences of the fighting were manifested experienced the war differently from those whose relationship to the war was one of distance and hearsay. Nurses, members of the middle- and upper-class Voluntary Aid Detachments (VADs), physicians at casualty clearing stations or base hospi-tals, or those who treated and cared for the wounded in hospitals in England; ambulance drivers transporting the wounded from battlefield to operating theater; individuals who served in auxiliary positions at the front or in support areas; YMCA and canteen volunteers in France; and those who underwent the traumas of war as victims of air raids or U-boat attacks; all represented their experiences of war in terms markedly dissimilar to those at home. While many of the images were also sexualized, the tone and content of the imagery conveyed a vastly different understanding of the relations of men and women in wartime, and this accounts, at least in part, for these individuals holding ideas about the nature of masculinity and femininity, and thus of feminism in the postwar period, that substantially differed from those of their colleagues.

Middle-class women in hospitals and at the front frequently commented upon the similarities they felt with the fighting men, evincing a solidarity or comradeship with them that overrode all distinctions. Upon taking up nursing, Vera Brittain constructed herself as in the same camp with fighting men, and as distinct from noncombatants. Her May 12, 1915 diary entry records her thoughts as she justified leaving Oxford to enter hospital training: 'I ought not to put the speedy starting of my career forward as an excuse, any more than a man should against enlisting,' she wrote. After her fiancé, Roland's, death, Brittain put in for foreign service, cognizant of the risks and dangers involved, but all the more adamant to go as a consequence. 'If I had refused to put down my name I should despise myself as much as I would a regiment that wouldn't volunteer for foreign service,' she explained. Once abroad, she shared with soldiers the sense of estrangement from the home front, 'the uncomprehending remoteness of England from the tragic, profound freemasonry of those who accepted death together overseas,' and spoke of those at home as 'the uninitiated.'[15] Mary Dexter, describing her uniform to her mother, noted with satisfaction the resemblance she and her fellow ambulance drivers had to army officers. She recounted that a French *poilu* had mistaken one of the drivers for a soldier during an air raid. 'In her greatcoat and cap and boots he had thought she was a man.'[16]

Sometimes the blurring of sexual difference became so intense as to eliminate even the physical markings that distinguished men's and women's bodies, as when Mary Borden described her nursing tour in base hospital in France. 'There are no men here,' she wrote of the patients she attended, 'so why should I be a woman?' 'I've never been so close before to human beings. We are locked together, the [orderlies] and I, and the wounded men; we are bound together.... The same thing is throbbing in us, the single thing, the one life. We are one body, suffering and bleeding.' After the war, Vera Brittain suffered from delusions that her face was changing; when she looked into a mirror, she believed she was 'developing a beard.'[17]

Women who encountered men at the front, whether they were wounded or not, experienced them in ways and formulated ideas about masculinity that differed markedly from those of the culture at home. In contrast to the image of the bloodthirsty soldiers who 'grin and kill and grin,' nurses and VADs described men in terms usually consigned to women and children, or in ways that denied them destructive power. An anonymous WAAC witnessed, in what she described as 'one of the most distressing sights that I beheld during the war,' a wounded man in her ambulance who 'began crying for his mother – "Oh, mummy, mummy, come to me – mummy, I want you so...." His voice was suddenly like a child's,' she wrote. A member of the First Aid Nursing Yeomanry (FANY) recalled that wounded men would 'burst into tears, refuse their food, beg to be allowed to stay,' when evacuation orders came for them. In vivid sketches evoking a mother–child relationship, Irene Rathbone's autobiographical protagonist, Joan, spoke of men 'unable to cut up their own food' who 'had to be spoon-fed,' of the patient to whom she brought a bed-pan, 'settled him comfortably upon it, [and] wiped him – if he were unable to manage himself.'[18] Often the wounded were referred to not as men but as broken objects or body parts. Cicely Hamilton reported that during her stint in France she 'grew quite accustomed to hearing human beings spoken of as if they were diseased or damaged portions of their bodies – as fractures or strangulated hernias.' Helen Zenna Smith's ambulance driver referred to 'these mangled things I drive night after night.' Borden observed of her ward that 'there are no men here.... There are heads and knees and mangled testicles. There are chests with holes as big as your fist, and pulpy thighs, shapeless; and stumps where legs once were fastened.... There are these things, but no men.'[19] Of course, this phenomenon of detaching the individual human being from the horrible wounds from which he suffered was a function of the women's need to survive and remain effective, but it also had the effect of separating men from the destructive forces that had occasioned their wounds.[20] Women at the front, unlike women at home, did not equate masculinity with brutality, aggression, and destruction. Rather, they perceived men as very much like children, or, indeed, like themselves.

Because the language used to express the experience of war at the front differed from that used to understand the war from the position of the home front, the sexual imagery necessarily differed as well. Rather than something to be feared or titillated by, sex, in the stories offered by the women at the front, offered pleasure, companionship, comfort, and love. Women frequently narrated their war experiences as a sexual coming-of-age, as tales depicting an unfolding of sexual knowledge that led, if not to actual sexual experience then to positive, relaxed attitudes about or openness towards sexuality. The stories all begin with an expression of more or less conventional Victorian attitudes toward and/or ignorance about sex. Vera Brittain's diary entries before the outbreak of war, for instance, reveal a sense of shame and even disgust about sex, what little she understood of it. When, in March 1913, on their way to play golf, she asked her mother 'to disclose a few points on sexual matters which I thought I ought to know,' she found the information so 'distasteful' and 'depressing' that it put her off her game. Joan, in *We That Were Young*, was also presented as a conventional middle-class Edwardian girl – earnest, innocent, and entirely ignorant about 'that mysterious consummation of love of which she had...on the whole kept resolutely from her thoughts.'[21]

Through contact with men's bodies in the course of their nursing duties the authors became accustomed to and then appreciative of the physical aspects of men. Until Vera Brittain began nursing in June 1915, she had 'never looked upon the nude body of an adult male.' At first she feared she would be overcome with nervousness and embarrassment at the sight of a naked man but found she was not. 'From the constant handling of their lean, muscular bodies, I came to understand the essential cleanliness, the innate nobility, of sexual love on its physical side,' she wrote. 'Although there was much to shock in Army hospital service, much to terrify, much, even, to disgust, this day-by-day contact with male anatomy was never part of the shame.' Irene Rathbone was also quite aware of the initiation into sexual knowledge she received from the soldiers under her care, describing the eroticism her protagonist, Joan, experienced when she bathed her patients.

> It gave her a peculiar soothing joy to take hold of a long white arm, to soap it, sponge it, and dry it; to wash a muscular young back, listening meanwhile to its owner talking desultorily about his sweetheart, his kids, or his 'mates' in the regiment. She was a nurse in uniform, and he was a wounded soldier; the gulf between them was fixed and rigid. And yet across that gulf, unrecognised and certainly unheeded by either, stretched the faint sweet fingers of sex.

Brittain shared that experience of sexual introduction, and appreciated it. She said of the wounded she nursed,

> Short of actually going to bed with them, there was hardly an intimate service that I did not perform for one or another in the course of four years, and I still have reason to be thankful for the knowledge of masculine functioning which the care of them gave me, and for my early release from the sex-inhibitions that even to-day [in 1933]...beset many of my female contemporaries, both married and single.[22]

Mary Borden utilized the sexual theme in a somewhat different way. Pain, 'a lascivious monster,' is portrayed in imagery usually associated with prostitution. She is

> insatiable, greedily, vilely amorous, lustful, obscene – she lusts for the broken bodies we have here. Wherever I go I find her possessing the men in their beds, lying in bed with them.... She is a harlot in the pay of War, and she amuses herself with the wreckage of men. She consorts with decay, is addicted to blood, cohabits with mutilations, and her delight is the refuse of suffering bodies.... You can watch her plying her trade here any day. She is shameless. She lies with the Heads and the Knees and the festering Abdomens. She never leaves them.... At any hour of the day or night you can watch her deadly amours, and watch her victims struggling.

This is also the kind of imagery utilized to portray the camp women enflamed by khaki fever at home, those furies preying upon the men in uniform, and whose licentious behavior is crippling the war effort and men's abilities to fulfill their masculine destiny. But for Borden the war itself is the whore, feeding on the once healthy bodies of men, rendering them grotesque and unnatural, and unfit for the 'tender and lovely love for women' that 'clean, normal, real men' seek. Having lost one of those 'clean, normal, real men' to the effects of amputation – 'she looked around her as if to find the man he had once been' – Borden turned to hospital work. Nurses and VADs, engaged in the battle that 'now is going on over the helpless bodies of these men,' 'we who are doing the fighting now, with their real enemies,' in this depiction are arrayed on the side of mutual, tender, loving, participatory sexual activity against a sexuality that is aggressive, predatory, diseased, and pecuniary. They do not win this fight, but Borden's story of her experience is none the less articulated in the same positive sexual terms as Brittain's and Rathbone's.

Women at the front or in positions that proximated those of the soldiers at the front shared with the men experiences denied to those at home. Rather than construe men in fantastic terms, derived from a different construction of war given in patriotic journalistic accounts, government propaganda, and sanitized letters home, feminists at the front had an understanding of men's daily lives and of men that was far more in keeping with those of the men themselves. We have seen that the sexual violation and mutilation of women by men served as one of the chief means by which to represent the war at home. Women at the front, by contrast, saw not the mutilation of women by men but the mutilation of men by the weapons of mass destruction unleashed by industrialized nations. Their familiarity with what men suffered led them to think of the male of the species not as some barbaric, destructive creature who could not control his most violent instincts, but as a hurt, pathetic, vulnerable, childlike victim of circumstances far beyond his control. The sexual imagery utilized to depict or represent the war, consequently, involved a much greater sense of partnership, of participation on equal terms, of fellowship with men, than did that of the home front. Whereas aggression and conflict characterized the sexual relations that were mobilized to depict the war at home, stories of sexual initiation, of awakening, of a sexual coming-of-age, predominated among the women at the front. These were described as affirming encounters with life lived at its fullest, though passion was often invoked. Comfort, caring, and giving, as opposed to conflict, violence, and destruction characterized the relations of men and women who shared the horrors and exigencies of war. These differing understandings about the nature of masculinity, and thus, given the dichotomies of male/female, of femininity, had important consequences in the postwar period as feminists began to formulate policies that turned on their conceptions of gender and sexuality.

'Old' feminists such as Winifred Holtby, Lady Rhondda, Cicely Hamilton, and Vera Brittain were able to hold on to understandings about masculinity and femininity, about male and female sexuality that characterized the prewar period. Their ability to contest the meanings about gender that were accepted not simply by the culture around them but by other feminists as well stems in part from the languages by means of which they articulated their experiences of the war.

While Hamilton, Brittain, and Borden viewed male aggression as largely a *learned* response, others – 'New' feminists – saw in the war a lesson about the *inherent* nature of masculinity, which led them to re-evaluate their beliefs about femininity as well. A number of feminists explicitly pointed to the war as the key event in effecting a transformation in their thinking. Catherine Gasquoine Hartley, for one, attributed her switch to what amounted to a 'new' feminist position to the massive male aggression manifested by the war. Whereas once she had dreamed of 'a golden age which was to come with the self-assertion of women,' with the outbreak of war, she explained in 1917, 'we women were brought back to the primitive conception of the relative position of the two sexes…. Again man was the fighter, the protector of woman and the home. And at once his power became a reality.' The aggression unleashed in the war, so unprecedented, so destructive, so horrifying in its effects, seems to have convinced Gasquoine Hartley that masculinity was essentially characterized by violence and brutality. Such an understanding necessitated that women, if they were ever to be really free, must accept

> the responsibilities and limitations of their womanhood. And by this I mean a full and glad acceptance of those physical facts of their organic constitution which make them unlike men, and should limit their capacity for many kinds of work. It can never be anything but foolishness to attempt to break down the real differences between the two sexes.

Christabel Pankhurst hinted of much the same fear when she wrote in 1924, 'Some of us hoped [for] more from woman suffrage than is ever going to be accomplished. My own large anticipations were based upon ignorance (which the late war dispelled) of the magnitude of the task which we women reformers so confidently wished to undertake when the vote should be ours.' Pankhurst's prewar writings made it clear that she sought in the vote the means by which women would end the sexual abuse and degradation of women. The realization that this would not be possible came to her as a result of her observation of the massive destruction of the Great War, the manifestation, for her as for so many others, of an innate male aggression. As she put it, 'war arises from passions and ambitions which do not yield to the influence of votes.'[23]

In these constructions, the metaphors of war had come home: the military had placed Britain, or at least the women of Britain, under military occupation. Where they had once conceived masculinity and femininity to be the products of laws, attitudes, and institutions that encouraged an unfettered and aggressive male sexuality and a passive, even nonexistent female sexuality, 'new' feminists now took up a variation of the 'drive–discharge' model that relied upon the notion of biological drives to explain male behavior. The social bases of masculinity and femininity gave way to a biologically determined, innate male and female sexuality, which in turn suggested that women must act differently in order to protect themselves and society from the aggression unleashed by war. The rhetoric of separate spheres had become infected with the rhetoric of war. In classic anti-feminist terms, these feminists gave voice to the cultural belief that the war had demonstrated the need for re-creating barriers between men and women, for the recognition of sexual difference, if society were to return to a condition of normality, defined in biological or natural terms. But because many of the legal barriers barring women from public life were being dismantled, the institutional practices enforcing separate spheres came to be replaced by psychological ones. The power of psychologized separate spheres, the extent of the psychic and linguistic internalization of military occupation by the women of Britain, insured that all the parliamentary reforms in the world would be of little avail to those seeking equality with men.

▶ New Feminism

These differing understandings, particularly about the nature of masculinity (and thus, given the dichotomies of male/female, of femininity) and the relationship between men and women, had important consequences as feminists began to formulate policies that turned on their conceptions of gender and sexuality. Organized feminism found itself splintered and constrained in its ability to advocate justice and equality for women by the gendered and highly sexualized languages used to represent the Great War. By the time war ended in 1918 masculinity and femininity had been construed in multiple and contradictory ways. In the first six months of the war, the idea of women as mothers, as givers of life, emerged from rhetoric that focused on women's roles in wartime and from arguments about the relationship of feminism and pacifism. It was accompanied, indeed, it depended upon, the notion of men as warriors, life-destroyers, and in the context of the Belgian atrocity stories, as bloodthirsty and rapacious. After 1915, as women flocked to munitions factories and auxiliary organizations, the predominant image of women as mothers gave way to that of women as warriors; in some representations, women could be seen as destroyers of men. Such a construction received strength from men who felt themselves emasculated by those at home who were responsible for prolonging the war, nearly always depicted as feminine, and, paradoxically, from women at the front who saw the broken bodies and heard the pitiable cries of men as they emerged from battle. The disparate, multiple representations of the war bode ill for a common postwar feminist vision of and rhetoric about the relationship between men and women and the reforms that would be derived therefrom.

The introduction and popularization of Freudian theory in the early 1920s offered both language and explanation for what had gripped the nations between 1914 and 1918. Freud himself was at least partly persuaded by the unprecedented violence of the war to elevate to the level of an instinct rivaling that of libido the tendency toward aggression. In 'Reflections upon War and Death,' written in 1915, Freud noted 'the brutality in behaviour shown by individuals, whom, as partakers in the highest form of human civilization, one would not have credited with such a thing.' What contemporaries believed to be 'evil tendencies' capable of being eradicated from society were, he explained, 'elemental instincts ... common to all men' that 'aim[ed] at the satisfaction of certain primal needs.' Individuals who behaved well in society, following the dictates of civilized culture, did not necessarily do so according to the 'dictates of their own natures.' Rather, in submitting to society's ideals and standards, they were vigorously suppressing their primitive instincts. The transformation of instincts demanded by culture was not necessarily permanent, and could be 'undone by the experiences of life. Undoubtedly,' Freud warned, 'the influences of war are among the forces that can bring about such regression.' In *Beyond the Pleasure Principle* and *The Ego and the Id*, published in 1920 and 1923, respectively, Freud's preoccupation with war and aggression found expression in his formulation of the notion of a death instinct that did battle with its opposite drive, Eros. In these works, he abandoned his earlier dichotomous pairing of drives – that of libido and ego. Aggression, Peter Gay observes, 'to which Freud had earlier devoted a measure of attention that he now deemed inadequate, became from 1920 on the equal adversary of Eros.'[24]

The pairing of Eros and Thanatos, of life and death, intimately linked sex and aggression. 'The aim of all life is death,' Freud declared, but the rush toward death is countered by the sexual instincts, 'the true life instincts.' When the drive toward death nears its completion, the drive toward life jerks it back and forces it to start anew. The opposition between the two resembled that between love (or affection) and hate (or aggression), what Freud had earlier called 'ambivalence of feeling.'[25] By 1923, with the publication of *The Ego and the Id*, Freud had come to believe that the two classes of instinct, the sexual instinct, or Eros, and the death instinct, represented by sadism, were 'fused, blended, and alloyed with each other,' ineradically intertwined. In fact, Freud claimed, it doesn't much matter which instinct is satisfied, 'so long as it takes place somehow,'[26] laying the groundwork for sexologists who would see in the satisfaction of the sexual impulse the solution to threats of war. Freud's ideas resonated in the minds and souls of the British, who had before the war not paid much, if any, attention to them. His theories about aggression most likely enabled many to understand and give expression to the experiences of the war years. What Elias Canetti remarked about Freud's reception in Vienna in the 1920s must hold true for London as well: 'What one had witnessed of murderous cruelty was unforgotten. Many who had participated actively had now returned. They knew well of what – on orders – they had been capable, and greedily caught hold of all the explanations for the predisposition to murder that psychoanalysis offered them.' By the time of Freud's popularization in Britain, the English could readily accept the notion that impulses towards sex and aggression were inter-twined with one another; indeed, many Britons held as 'a deeply rooted cultural assumption' the view of war as a release from long-suppressed libidinal energies. Caroline Playne wrote in 1931, in a book investigating 'the psychological states which, all must agree, were at the back of the great upheaval' of 1914–1918, that 'the madness of the war years must be conceived as the madness of men' driven by 'the primitive lust of getting the best of those you hate.' She spoke of 'a bout of overflowing national lust,' a phenomenon that was clearly sexual in nature, as indicated by her allusions to 'the tidal floods of life [that] were inundating, fertil-izing the dry lands of human civilization,' to 'the engines of life' and 'the flood of passion.'[27]

The intimate cultural associations of sex and war made it possible for sexolo-gists to theorize and present to the public the notion that sexual relations between men and women resembled war, and to exploit this reification of warlike erotic 'instincts' to establish the power and legitimacy of their profession. This devel-opment would have a significant impact upon the thinking of those involved in theorizing about the relations between men and women, particularly physicians, psychiatrists and sexologists, and feminists, many of whom embraced the conser-vative images of femininity and masculinity that arose as British society sought in the establishment of harmonious marital relationships a resolution to the anxieties and political turmoil caused by the Great War. Britons, including feminists, looked to create peace and order in the public sphere of social, economic, and political relations by imposing peace and order on the private sphere of sexual relations.

The inscription of large societal anxieties and conflicts onto marital relationships operated on at least two levels. On the one hand, gender, sexuality, and the rela-tionship between the sexes served as metaphors through which issues of power might be resolved by referring to notions of sexual difference. On the other hand, sexuality and war were understood by the culture – consciously or unconsciously – to be inextricably intertwined. Thus, the resolution of conflict through mutual, pleasurable sexual experiences within marriage was regarded by many sexologists and sex reformers as a means of reducing the threat of war by removing the sexual repressions and tensions that, they sometimes implied, helped to bring it about.[28] The discourses on sexuality that predominated in the postwar years appropriated the language and imagery of war as psychoanalysts, sexologists, and sex reformers sought in the study of sexuality the solutions to the maintenance and salvation of civilization itself. As Havelock Ellis, the most influential sexologist in interwar Britain, wrote in *The Psychology of Sex*, his popular textbook, sex 'is not merely the channel along which the race is maintained and built up, it is the foundation on which all dreams of the future world must be erected.' For Ellis, as for all 'scientists of sex' in the 1920s and 1930s, sexual activity was firmly located within marriage, and its chief and central aim, after the carnage wrought by the Great War, was procreation. A more insistent ideology of motherhood demanded that women leave their wartime jobs, give up their independence, and return to home and family, where their primary occupation – their obligation, in fact – would be the bearing and rearing of children.[29]

If the sexual disorder of war was to be followed by peace, the metaphor required sexual peace, a model of marital accord achieved through mutual sexual enjoyment. Discourses about female sexuality which before the war had emphasized women's lack of sexual impulse, and even distaste for sexual intercourse, underwent modification to accommodate the political, social, and economic requirements of the postwar period. The new accent on motherhood was accompanied by a growing emphasis on the importance of sexual activity, sexual pleasure, and sexual compatibility between husband and wife.[30] Women denied sexual pleasure in marriage might easily transform their hunt for love into a hatred for the entire male sex, Theodore Van de Velde warned. Men, because they could masturbate to relieve sexual tension, ran a far less risk of 'thus turning against the whole female sex.'[31]

As marriage and marital sex bore the brunt of restoring social harmony in postwar Britain, sex manuals – how-to guides to conjugal fulfillment – became bestsellers. Marie Stopes's *Married Love*, published in 1918, sold more than 2000 copies in the first two weeks, and 400,000 by 1923. Theodore Van de Velde's *Ideal Marriage, Its Physiology and Technique* (1926) went through 43 printings. Such books as Isabel Emslie Hutton's *The Sex Technique in Marriage* (1932), Helena Wright's *The Sex Factor in Marriage*, and Van de Velde's *Sex Hostility in Marriage* (1931) attest to the broadly perceived need to establish sexual peace through sexual pleasure. Of Stopes's *Married Love*, Mary Stocks wrote that 'this book with its spectacular sales brought more happiness to more people than any other publication of our time.' Van de Velde's *Sex Hostility in Marriage* sought to 'help those numerous people, whose happiness is menaced by the spectre of hostility in marriage to combat this danger.... Few married couples are aware of the evil and dangerous enemy that stands so near to them.' The imagery of war – 'combat,' Van de Velde's 'attacks' on the 'enemy,' – testify to the heavy load sex was being asked to carry. Domestic harmony, and thus social peace, appeared to Britons to depend upon the establishment of a managed and controlled sexuality whereby warriors could be rendered peacelike and wherein women could find, acknowledge, and express their sexuality within a framework of 'scientific' approbation.[32]

And, as we saw in chapter 1, interwar sexologists, psychologists, and psychoanalysts regarded women who refused marriage and motherhood as distorted, even diseased creatures. The description of feminists as abnormal, sexually maladjusted women who hated men and the equating of feminism with sex war were not, of course, new, but the context in which such charges were leveled was entirely different now. The existence of large numbers of unmarried women produced a great deal of anxiety. The diatribes directed at them reflected society's longing to return to the familiar, 'traditional' ways of life before August 1914, a nostalgic projection that failed to recall the way life 'really' was in Edwardian times. Denied husbands, many of them, by the destruction of the Great War, single women were visible reminders of the war that had only recently ended. Feminism soon became linked in the public mind not merely with sex war, a somewhat familiar concept, but with armed conflict, death, and destruction. Arabella Kenealy, a lecturer at the Royal College of Physicians in Dublin, argued in 1920 in a book pointedly titled *Feminism and Sex-Extinction* that

> men and women are naturally dependent upon one another in every human relation; a dispensation which engenders reciprocal trust, affection and comradeship. Feminist doctrine and practice menace these most excellent previsions and provisions of Nature by thrusting personal rivalries, economic competition and general conflict of interests between the sexes.

She urged women to recognize the inevitability of sex differences and to give up their wartime jobs to men, explaining that men would use violence against them if they refused to vacate their positions. After the horrific events of the Great War, the specter of conflict between men and women could hardly be tolerated; postwar society sought above all to re-establish a sense of peace and security in an unfamiliar and very insecure world. The insistence upon gender peace – a relationship of complementarity between men and women in which women did not compete with men in the public sphere, and thereby provoke men to anger, the world as envisaged by anti-feminists – appears to have been the most fundamental step in that direction. Prewar feminism, with its suggestion of sex war, seems to have become associated in the public mind with a renewal of the massive conflict so recently ended.

Feminists participated in the cultural linking of sexual disharmony and the threat of war. F.W. Stella Browne, writing in 1915, utilized the rhetoric of war in her argument for recognizing 'Sexual Variety and Variability among Women, and their Bearing upon Social Reconstruction' after the war, claiming that 'much of the unhealthiness of sexual conditions at present, is due to the habit of segregating the sexes in childhood and partly in latter life, and making them into "alien enemies" to one another.' Elizabeth Robins believed that sex antagonism 'is the seed of all the other Antagonisms that ravage the earth. You shall not deal faithfully with any other till you have dealt faithfully with that.'[33] Many, echoing the sexologists, saw in sex the salvation of civilization. Stella Browne, in very much the same imagery that Freud and sexologists would conjure up after the war, warned of 'very dangerous and degrading perversions which may develop under repression. I know of a case in which a sudden, inexplicable, but apparently irresistible, lust of cruelty developed in a woman of the most actively kind and tender heart, but... sexually unsatisfied.' Rebecca West warned of the ongoing nature of sex antagonism, stating that 'in this war there is no discharge' for 'such of the sexes as are not intimately in harmony.' Dora Russell's *Hypatia* (1925) opened with a statement that equated marital discord with war. 'Matrimonial quarrels, like modern war,' she asserted, 'are carried on on a large scale, involving not individuals, nor even small groups of individuals, but both sexes and whole classes of society.' Russell was one of the few feminists in the postwar period willing to speak about hostility between women and men; she saw in sexual reform the 'way out of the intolerable tangle in which their quarreling has landed us.' 'To understand sex,' she promised, 'to bring to it dignity and beauty and knowledge born of science, in place of brute instinct and squalor – that is the bridge that will span the breach between' the sexes.[34]

And not just the sexes. In many of her writings Russell articulated some of the misgivings about equal-rights feminism that haunted the proponents of 'new' feminism: that by insisting upon equality with men, by competing with men in the marketplace, equal rights feminists threatened to undo the international peace. In chapter 1 of *Hypatia*, which is subtitled, 'Is there a Sex War?' Russell conceded that, owing to women's rebellion against 'a system of masculine repression,' there had indeed been one. 'It was a disgraceful exhibition,' she observed, slipping into an equation of feminism and the Great War, 'and would not have come to a truce so soon, but that it was eclipsed by the still more disgraceful exhibition of the European war.' Completing the metonymy, she concluded, 'In 1918 they bestowed the vote... as a reward for our services in helping the destruction of our offspring.' Wholly sympathetic to the cause, Russell nevertheless gave voice to a widespread understanding of feminism as war: 'Feminism led women away from the home that they might return armed and unsubdued to make marriage tolerable,' she declared. Mutual sexual pleasure, she believed, offered a solution not only to antagonism between men and women, but to conflict between nations as well. 'I think that through sex and through parenthood we might get people away from admiration of a social system built on war,' she told a Guildhouse audience. More explicitly, she argued in *The Right to Be Happy* that in sex-love, through physical sympathy and intimate union, we draw into ourselves as in no other way the understanding of another human personality, and the knowledge that two very different creatures can live together in exquisite harmony. Such an experience alone, widespread, would be worth ten million platforms blaring pacifism.[35]

Feminists' conceptions of gender and sexuality were powerfully influenced by the conservative and reactionary images of masculinity and femininity that emerged in the postwar period, as British society sought in the establishment of harmonious marital relationships a resolution to the anxieties and political turmoil caused by the Great War. Just as nineteenth-century physicians and scientists had created sexual discourses that upheld a particular social and gender system by establishing the political identity of individuals on the basis of their sexuality, twentieth-century psychiatrists, sexologists, and sex reformers built up a vast literature about masculinity and femininity and male and female sexuality that served to restore order in the face of dramatic upheavals in the political, economic, social, and gender structures of Britain. A gender system of separate spheres for men and women based upon scientific theories of sexual difference, a new emphasis upon motherhood, and an urgent insistence upon mutual sexual pleasure within marriage provided parameters within which 'normal' activity was to be carried out and a return to normalcy effected.[36] Most feminists, no less interested in the establishment of peace and order, adopted these discourses as they articulated their demands. 'New' feminism failed to challenge, and in fact contributed to, a reconstruction of gender that circumscribed the roles, activities, and possibilities of women. In so doing, it abandoned the radical critiques of gender and sexuality that marked its prewar ideologies, critiques that had probably become anachronistic, irrelevant to the discourses that predominated in postwar Britain.

Prewar feminists could assert women's independence and equality of the sexes in the conviction that they would ultimately ensure a better world for both women and men. The traumas of the Great War, and the imagery by which they were represented, undermined this belief. Violence, war, and conflict could only be avoided, it appeared to British society after 1918, by redrawing separate spheres for men and women, not now necessarily marked as public and private by laws and institutional practices that had barred women from public life in the past. A psychologized version of separate spheres, one consequence of depicting war in the imagery of sexual violence, and of postwar sexological and psychoanalytic discourses that represented sexual relations in the imagery of war, proved to be just as effective in limiting women's scope and agency as barriers between public and private spheres had been in the past. 'New' feminism, by accepting the terms of the larger culture, by putting forward an uncritical politics of sexual difference, found itself severely constrained in its ability to advocate equality and justice for women.

Conclusion: Where We Go From Here

In December 2008, the *American Historical Review* published a forum entitled 'Revisiting "Gender: A Useful Category of Historical Analysis." '[1] In it, a number of historians of the United States, Latin America, Eastern Europe, medieval Europe, and China spoke about the impact Scott's article had had on their own work on gender and that of their fields generally. The pieces testified to quite a bit of variety in the reception and usages of gender as an analytic category, but all of them acknowledged how important Scott's theorizing had been for them and their sub-disciplines.

In her own contribution to the forum, Scott demurred, insisting that she had not inaugurated any new approach. She had only put together in one place what feminists in a number of fields were talking about. 'I was giving voice to – not inventing – some of the ideas and questions that the feminist movement had posed, looking for ways to turn political questions into historical ones,' she claimed.[2] Well, maybe only that, but Scott is too modest here. In putting these ideas together in exactly the way she did when she did, she busted open not just gender history, but history generally.

Scott noted that the forum articles gave witness to how powerful gender had turned out to be in the analysis of power as it showed up in places like war, empire, state formation, nation-building and nationalism, racism, revolution, economics, and finance – you name it, there it was. After all, as she had posited 22 years earlier, 'gender is a primary way of signifying power' and 'gender constructs politics.' She was less sanguine about the counter-claim she had made about how 'politics constructs gender,' lamenting the general lack of historical studies that treated that side of the equation. She urged scholars to look again at Denise Riley's *'Am I That Name?' Feminism and the Category of 'Women' in History* as a model for the questions gender historians might raise, exhorting them to take up 'the unfinished business of the transformation in historical consciousness that the "Gender" article has come to signify.'[3] She called for a history of the category of 'women' that would subject all elements of sexed identities – including sexuality – to questioning. Did the seemingly eternal opposition of male/female, masculine/feminine binary really operate that way throughout history? She pointed out that Riley had regarded that apparently fixed binary as itself a historical construction – if that is so, where do we see something other than fixed binaries constructing gender, and what are the political implications of such an arrangement?

Let me suggest one possible answer to that question, put forward in a book co-authored by Misty Bastian, an anthropologist, Marc Matera, a historian, and me. It's called *The Women's War of 1929: Gender and Violence in Colonial Nigeria*. In it, the three of us analyze one of the most remarkable events in African and British colonial history, when, in November and December 1929, a dramatic series of demonstrations, protests, risings, and riots involving tens of thousands of Igbo- and Ibibio-speaking women took place throughout southeastern Nigeria. The 'Aba Riots,' as the British dubbed them at the time, in what was on one level a bid to efface their extraordinary nature, were known to their participants and to subsequent West African memory and historiography as the *Ogu Umunwaanyi*, 'the Women's War.' In the course of it, over 50 Igbo and Ibibio women were killed by British troops and an unknown number were wounded and otherwise traumatized.[4] We examine the various perspectives of the main protagonists in a single, gendered analytical frame.

Earlier treatments of the Women's War have seen its causes in economic or political grievance. We argue that the political and economic factors that gave rise to the *Ogu Umunwaanyi* cannot be separated from larger Igbo and other southeastern social systems, especially the gender system that governed people's lives, which were being transformed by and reacting to their engagement with the tenets of colonial, western society. Pre- and early colonial Igbo-speaking peoples possessed a highly developed religious cosmology rooted in their historical experience of the material world as well as in their many moral precepts and understandings of 'the sacred.' A first and important Igbo cosmological concept – one that remained elusive for the British in their interaction with Igbo-speakers – concerned the *continuity* and *contiguity* (as opposed to the polarity) of all parts of the cosmos. The 'great spirit' Chukwu, the living, and the dead intermingled and existed in the same conceptual space, even while they all inhabited special spheres. Although Igbo-speakers regarded Chukwu and Ala/Ani, the land, as being prior and therefore senior to humanity, humanity partook of both spiritual forces. During conception, for instance, Chukwu 'furnishes part of his own substance, "chi," to the human child.'[5] Every human being, then, contained a part of Chukwu, while also being given a physical body by his or her parents. However, upon death, the form (*onunu*) of each child (derived from Ala, the land) and the body returned to the land for that form's dissolution. The ancestors, both paternal and maternal, held a stake in the child through the Igbo concept of reincarnation. Any ancestor – and, indeed, although more rarely, people from outside the kin group – might manifest himself or herself in any child. Men could therefore be reincarnated as females; women as males. Following recent scholarship on the ambiguity of African gender systems,[6] it is clear that Igbo speakers who could reincarnate in a variety of genders and even as non-human beings operated within a different gender ideology than that informing western societies. The key to a successful life involved taking on the responsibilities of one's current gender status in a mature and committed manner. Being successful, in gendered as well as other social terms, entailed being 'useful.'[7]

Although the Igbo recognized the individual and what contemporary theorists would call her agency as being important (note, for instance, that every person has her own personal *chi*, which directs her fortunes in the world of the living), that individual person was most *socially* important insofar as her attainments benefited some larger group. Whether the group constituted the individual's kin group – in its extension to both the living and the dead – or his or her village, Igbo beliefs recognized that every person's achievement had the potential to benefit everyone else. Collective action provided, or should have provided, the means by which people 'got up' or helped their village or market to 'get up.'[8] A woman going to market, for instance, depended upon her children to help her sell her goods; a young man involved in studying at a university depended upon the financial and moral support of his entire village.[9] The children of the woman trader expected, rightly, to benefit from their mother's success, as she was often the person who paid their school fees and fed them. The village expected both tangible rewards – in the form of a sharing of the benefits given to the educated elite – and less apparent ones – in the form of prestige and village honor.

This ethic of mutual benefit applied also to gender relations across southeastern Nigeria, but particularly among Igbo speakers. Although wives were said to be 'owned'[10] by their husbands, and their children belonged to the man's patriline, women tended to operate in a fairly independent manner. Every precolonial Igbo wife, for example, was supposed to have her own house within the husband's compound and was responsible mainly to herself for her comings and goings outside the compound walls. In addition to sexual service, wives in the precolonial and early colonial period owed their husbands meals – which every wife cooked and presented for the husband to taste, he deciding which wife's meal he would actually consume. Men were obligated to provide their wives with yams to cook and clothes to wear: 'It is the husband's duty to provide the staple crops – yams, maize, beans – and the wife's duty to provide the ingredients for soup, condiments, water and fuel, and to see that the cooking is properly done.'[11] Beyond these basics, women had to fend for themselves – and usually did so quite capably.

Precolonial Igbo worldviews involved, then, a series of systems of mutual interdependence. Even conception required an effort of mutual cooperation – not just between men and women, but between the human world and the spirit world and even between the living and the dead. The absence of consent on the part of any party 'renders conception impossible.'[12] Chukwu gave the person his or her spirit;

Ala/Ani gave the person his or her form; one of the dead had to be willing to be reincarnated (*iluo uwa*);[13] and a couple had to come together sexually to make the physical stuff of human bodies. Precolonial Igbo people expected to find this mutual interdependence in virtually every realm of life: in the political arena, in their ultimate control over anyone they chose to put into office, for example, and in their domestic affairs, where the mundane practice of activities like cooking carried significant symbolic valence. Men supplied basic and highly valued foodstuffs, but women controlled their preparation and gave food savor through their use of condiments and extra vegetables from 'women's crops.' Just as no pounded yam, a great favorite among the Igbo, could be prepared without male input (i.e., the yam itself), the starch staple would not be good to eat without women's laborious pounding and the pepper sauce they created to pour over it.

When every individual contributed – and that included the expressly gendered deities – the whole benefited. Problems occurred when any one element of a partnership tried to benefit more than the other parts, or, as the Igbo proverb has it, '*Mmadu bu nso ala*' ('human beings spoil the land').[14] In such cases, the balance had to be restored, as the withdrawal of any party from these systems of interdependence endangered all other parties and all other systems. An abomination to the land affected the fertility of humans and crops because Ala then had reason to withdraw from the cause of the abomination (i.e., from all humans). This, in turn, affected human interaction because people withdrew from each other if they were seen as somehow sterile or the cause of *alulu ani* (the act of causing abomination). The *ndichie* withdrew from the unharmonious human community of the living and were affected by Ala's withdrawal, as she was their 'mother' just as she was the 'mother' of the living, and she included in her cosmographic domains the land of the dead.

At the most extreme end of the dissolution of social ties, chaos reigned, and even Chukwu might withdraw, leaving only his servant, death, in his wake. The withdrawal of Chukwu constituted the ultimate danger in Igbo cosmological thought, because his withdrawal must signify the withdrawal of his substance, the *chi* that gave life to every individual. Cosmological systems of mutual interdependence and the relations between those systems in the precolonial Nigerian southeast had to be maintained. Without the interplay of worlds, the entire Igbo cosmos might collapse and all human beings would die, becoming like those barren or abominated people denied existence in the land of the dead and subsequent re-entry into the land of the living. Such an eventuality was understood to be what westerners might call catastrophically traumatic, as its effects would be lasting and non-recuperative.

British actions that led to the outbreak of the Women's War in 1929 and the reactions of colonial officials to the disturbances derived from a worldview in which gender played out in an entirely different framework. Like virtually all stories westerners told themselves about the way the world worked, the British imaginary about

Africa depended upon the creation of distinct binary opposites for its structure and comprehension: of civilization versus 'the wilds,' of morality versus savagery, of reason versus superstition, of north versus south, and of order versus chaos. In each instance, gender often served to represent these binaries, sexuality to articulate their manifestations. Such a Manichaean meaning system, based on gender and sexuality, confronting the cosmologies of West African peoples, informed by their own understandings of gender and sexuality, set the stage for the conflict that erupted at the end of 1929. For by that time, the meanings attached to gender by the British in the purportedly all-male world of the colonial state of Nigeria ascribed to southern provinces a 'messiness' associated with femininity that had attained dangerous proportions.

Africa and Africans, in the minds of the British, signified unalterable, fundamental difference from European social and gender roles, European morals, mores, customs, values, and traditions; these differences were usually expressed by means of a disordered gender system and promiscuous sexuality attributed to Africans, and especially to African women, by writers and explorers. These kinds of descriptions reduced Africans and African societies to the level of primitive savagery, a state of being that excused British involvement in the slave trade on the grounds that Africans could hardly be counted as human. When the British outlawed the slave trade in 1807 and then slavery itself in British territories in 1833, these same depictions of Africans as bestial were drawn upon to justify later nineteenth- and twentieth-century British efforts to subdue and control the peoples of Africa by an imperial rule that promised to raise them up to 'civilized' status.

The colonial encounter generated borrowings and adaptations of aspects of each gendered worldview, but they also produced a continuous series of misrecognition of actions and intentions. Southeastern Nigerian women assumed that British officials would comprehend their actions, acknowledging that their grievances were readily apparent and just. The British lacked the conceptual apparatus to recognize the women's behavior as an explicitly gendered, political performance. Failure to do so culminated in profound acts of violence. *The Women's War* brings together the actions and thinking of the women of the *Ogu* and those of the British officers and colonial officials involved in the events of 1929. It describes and explains how southeastern Nigerian women and Britons believed the world worked, and how gender operated within their respective worldviews. It is only by appreciating how their differing worldviews animated the actors' clashes with one another that we can fully grasp the meaning of the *Ogu* within the context of the British colonial and the indigenous imaginations.

The juxtaposition of the universe within which southeastern Nigerian women operated against that of the other major participants in this 'women's movement' – British colonial, missionary, and mercantile actors – yields compelling insights about the actions of all parties involved. In their broad strokes, ideas about and understandings of gender on the part of all the actors in the Women's War were incommensurate on several levels. At certain moments in certain situations, certain actors transcended the confines of their respective worldviews, but for the most part British and indigenous West African peoples found themselves talking across a chasm of misrecognition. A historical ethnography of both the colonized and the colonizers reminds us that gender is not universal, natural, or static, but rather articulates meaning systems particular to each.[15] Western concepts of gender map onto sexual difference, and assume a whole host of binaries, especially that of a public/private split for men and women; they often present relations between men and women as a battlefield from which one gender must necessarily emerge victorious, and regard victory in terms of privileges associated with masculinity in European and North American society. These binary constructions have distorted our understanding of the women's actions. Because westerners have difficulty accepting what appear to be contradictions in the lives of southeastern Nigerian women, the filter of western gender obscures our appreciation that they could be completely at home in their personae as women traders and the guardians of the good of the land as well as in their personae as daughters, wives and mothers. Not thinking of themselves as oppressed or kept in what used to be called 'the domestic sphere' – like their female counterparts in western societies even in quite recent history – these women could be secure enough in their own sense of importance and worth to take an active part in social transformation, to try to effect change, and even to see advantages for themselves in change that was properly regulated.

As I hope I have conveyed in the course of this book, gender history has transformed our discipline. Even the most inveterate old-fashioned historians must acknowledge the importance of gender for their work, even if they do then leave it aside for the rest of the book. Those who take it seriously – who grapple with the questions about identity, subjectivity, materiality, knowledge production, and power relations it demands we address – have produced extraordinarily insightful studies. I have written this book to familiarize you with the various theories that undergird gender history in hopes of providing you with the tools you might use to go out and write histories of your own. It's hard to do, there is no question about it, but it will prove to be one of the most gratifying activities of your life.

Notes

▶ Introduction: Gender: What Is It? Who Has It?

1 See Bonnie G. Smith, *The Gender of History: Men, Women, and Historical Practice* (Cambridge, MA, 1998).

2 See Joan W. Scott, 'Gender: A Useful Category of Historical Analysis,' *American Historical Review* 91:5 (December 1986): 1053–75; and Joanne Meyerowitz, 'A History of "Gender,"' in *AHR Forum*: 'Revisiting "Gender: A Useful Category of Historical Analysis,"' *American Historical Review* 113:5 (December 2008): 1346–56.

▶ 1 Woman: From the Imperfect Male to the Incommensurate Female

1 Confucius, 'The Analects,' in Alfred Andrea and James Overfield, eds., *The Human Record: Sources in Global History*, Vol. I (3rd ed., Boston, 1998), pp. 96–9.

2 Marguerite Deslauriers, 'Sexual Difference in Aristotle's Politics and His Biology,' *Classical World* 102:3 (Spring 2009): 215–31.

3 Quoted in Thomas Laqueur, *Making Sex: Body and Gender from the Greeks to Freud*, (Cambridge, MA, 1990), p. 25.

4 Quoted in Laqueur, *Making Sex*, p. 28.

5 Quoted in Laqueur, *Making Sex*, p. 59.

6 Quoted in Laqueur, *Making Sex*, p. 64.

7 Laqueur, *Making Sex*, p. 150.

8 See Susan Kingsley Kent, *Sex and Suffrage in Britain, 1860–1914* (Princeton, NJ, 1987), ch. 2.

9 Quoted in Jeffrey Weeks, *Sex, Politics and Society: The Regulation of Sexuality Since 1800* (London, 1981), pp. 154–5.

10 Sigmund Freud, 'The Dissolution of the Oedipus Complex,' quoted in Peter Gay, *Freud, A Life for Our Time* (New York, 1988), p. 515: 'There was nothing in the climate of the 1920s and nothing in Freud's psychological biography to prompt the revisions that would make him propound his controversial, at times

scurrilous, views on woman.' Sigmund Freud, 'Some Psychological [*sic*] Consequences of the Anatomical Distinction Between the Sexes,' 1925, in Philip Rieff, ed., *Sexuality and the Psychology of Love* (New York, 1963), pp. 187, 188, 191, 193.

11 A. Costler, A. Willy, et al.; Norman Haire, general editor, *Encyclopaedia of Sexual Knowledge* (New York, 1940; English ed., 1934), pp. 288–9.

12 Theodore H. Van de Velde, *Sex Hostility in Marriage: Its Origin, Prevention and Treatment* (London, 1931), pp. 30, 43, 68–9, 120, 66. Karl Abraham, 'Manifestations of the Female Castration Complex' (1920), in Jean Strouse, ed., *Women and Analysis: Dialogues on Psychoanalytic Views of Femininity* (New York, 1974), p. 139. Havelock Ellis, *Sex in Relation to Society: Studies in the Psychology of Sex*, Vol. 6 (1946), quoted in Sheila Jeffreys, *The Spinster and Her Enemies: Feminism and Sexuality 1800–1930*, (North Melbourne, 1997), p. 137.

13 Quoted in Sheila Jeffreys, 'Sex Reform and Anti-feminism in the 1920s,' in London Feminist History Group, *The Sexual Dynamics of History* (Pluto Press, London, 1983), pp. 185, 190. K.A. Weith Knudsen, *Feminism: The Woman Question from Ancient Times to the Present Day* (London, 1928), quoted in Jeffreys, *The Spinster and Her Enemies*, p. 176. Quoted in ibid., p. 12. Quoted in Jeffreys, 'Sex Reform and Anti-feminism,' p. 199.

▶ 2 'One is not born a woman': The Feminist Challenge

1 Quoted in ibid., ch. 7.

2 Simone de Beauvoir, *The Second Sex* (New York, 1953), 'Introduction.'

3 See Barbara Caine, *English Feminism, 1780–1980* (Oxford, 1997), 'Afterword.'

4 Hilary Rose, 'Women's Work: Women's Knowledge,' in Juliet Mitchell and Ann Oakley, eds., *What is Feminism? A Re-examination* (New York, 1986), p. 161.

5 Dale Spender, *Women of Ideas (and What Men have Done to Them)* (London, 1982), pp. 4–5.

6 Quoted in Caine, *English Feminism*, p. 266.

7 This section is taken from Susan Kingsley Kent, *Sex and Suffrage in Britain, 1860–1914* (Princeton, NJ, 1987), chs. 3, 5, and 7.

8 Shulasmith Firestone, *The Dialectic of Sex: The Case for Feminist Revolution* (New York, 1970).

9 Gayle Rubin, 'The Traffic in Women: Notes on the "Political Economy" of Sex,' in Rayna R. Reiter, *Toward and Anthropology of Women* (New York, 1975), p. 204.

10 Quoted in Sara Evans, *Born for Liberty: A History of Women in America* (New York, 1989), p. 297.

11 Beverley Bryan, Stella Dadzie, and Suzanne Scafe, *The Heart of the Race: Black Women's Lives in Britain* (London, 1985), p. 147.

12 Ibid., pp. 149–50.

13 Hazel Carby, 'White Woman Listen! Black Feminism and the Boundaries of Sisterhood,' in Centre for Contemporary Cultural Studies, *The Empire Strikes Back: Race and Racism in 70s Britain* (London, 1982), pp. 213, 221.

▶ 3 The Road to 'Gender'

1 See Bonnie G. Smith, *The Gender of History: Men, Women, and Historical Practice* (Cambridge, MA, 1998), and Mary Spongberg, *Writing Women's History since the Renaissance* (New York, 2002).

2 There is a vast, vast literature here. See, just for starters, Sheila Rowbotham, *Hidden from History* (London, 1973) and *Women's Consciousness, Man's World* (London, 1973); Gerda Lerner, *The Majority Finds Its Past* (New York, 1979). For the United States, see Ellen DuBois, *Feminism and Suffrage: The Emergence of an Independent Women's Movement in America* (Ithaca, NY, 1978); Alice Kessler-Harris, *Out to Work: A History of Wage-Earning Women in the United States* (New York, 1982). For Britain, see Sally Alexander, 'Women, Class and Sexual Difference: Some Reflections on the Writing of Feminist History,' *History Workshop Journal* 17 (Spring 1984): 125–49; Leonore Davidoff, 'Mastered for Life: Servant and Wife in Victorian and Edwardian England,' *Journal of Social History* 7 (1973–4): 406–28. For France, see Bonnie G. Smith, *Ladies of the Leisure Class: The Bourgeoises of Northern France* (Princeton, NJ, 1981). For Australia, see Norma Grieve and Patricia Grimshaw, eds., *Australian Women: Feminist Perspectives* (Melbourne, 1981); Miriam Dixson, *The Real Matilda: Women and Identity in Australia* (Ringwood, AU, 1975); Anne Summers, *Damned Whores and God's Police: The Colonization of Women in Australia* (Ringwood, AU, 1975); Beverly Kingston, *My Wife, My Daughter and Poor Mary Ann: Women and Work in Australia* (West Melbourne, 1975); Edna Ryan and Anne Conlon, *Gentle Invaders: Women at Work in Australia, 1788–1974* (Melbourne, 1975); Anne Curthoys, Susan Eade, and Peter Spearritt, eds., *Women at Work* (Melbourne, 1975).

3 Sheila Rowbotham, 'The Trouble with Patriarchy'; Sally Alexander and Barbara Taylor, 'In Defence of "Patriarchy,"' *New Statesman*, December 1979. Sue Morgan, ed., Introduction, *The Feminist History Reader* (London, 2006), p. 6. Judith Bennett, 'Feminism and History,' *Gender and History* 1:3 (1989): 251–72.

4 Barbara Welter, 'The Cult of True Womanhood,' *American Quarterly* 18 (1966): 151–74.

5 Carroll Smith-Rosenberg, 'The Female World of Love and Ritual: Relations Between Women in Nineteenth Century America,' *Signs* 1:1 (1975): 1–18.

6 Joan Wallach Scott, 'Women in History: The Modern Period,' *Past and Present* 101 (November 1983): 141–57, pp. 148, 149, 150, 152.

7 Her paper was published as ' "Women's History" in Transition: The European Case,' *Feminist Studies* 3:3–4 (1976): 83–103, p. 90.

8 Joan Kelly-Gadol, 'The Social Relation of the Sexes: Methodological Implications of Women's History,' *Signs* 1:4 (Summer 1976): 809–23, p. 817.

9 Quoted in Jane Rendall, ' "Uneven Developments": Women's History, Feminist History and Gender History in Great Britain,' in Karen M. Offen, Ruth Roach, and Jane Rendall, eds., *Writing Women's History: International Perspectives* (Bloomington, IN, 1991), pp. 45–57, p. 49.

10 See Amanda Vickery, 'Golden Age to Separate Spheres? A Review of the Categories and Chronology of English Women's History,' *Historical Journal* 36:2 (1993): 26–64; Laura Lee Downs, *Writing Gender History* (London, 2004).

11 Joan Wallach Scott, 'Gender: A Useful Category of Historical Analysis,' *American Historical Review* 91:5 (1986): 1053–75, p. 1057.

12 This explanation comes from Terry Eagleton, *Literary Theory: An Introduction* (Minneapolis, 1996), via Phil Deloria, whose precision of thought and expression I rely on heavily to explain all this. Phil generously allowed me to take this language from a book on how to do cultural studies we are writing together.

13 This discussion of postmodernism relies upon the great clarity of Jane Flax in *Thinking Fragments: Psychoanalysis, Feminism, and Postmodernism in the Contemporary West* (Berkeley, CA, 1990).

14 See ibid., p. 5.

15 Scott, 'Gender: A Useful Category of Historical Analysis,' p. 1067.

16 See Michel Foucault, *Discipline and Punish: The Birth of the Prison*(trans. Alan Sheridan, New York, 1977); *The Birth of the Clinic: An Archaeology of Medical Perception* (trans. A.M. Sheridan Smith, New York, 1973); *The History of Sexuality, Volume I: An Introduction* (trans. Robert Hurley, New York, 1978); *Madness and Civilization: A History of Insanity in the Age of Reason* (trans. Richard Howard, New York, 1965).

17 Scott, 'Gender: A Useful Category of Historical Analysis,' p. 1068.

▶ **4 Theorizing Gender and Power**

1 Gisela Bock, 'Women's History and Gender History: Aspects of an International Debate,' *Gender and History* 1:1 (Spring, 1989): 7–30, p. 17.

2 See Alain Corbin, *Les filles de noces: Misère sexuelle et prostitution aux XiXe et XXe siècles* (Paris, 1978), Corbin, 'Le "sexe-en-deuil" et l'histoire des femmes au XIXe siècle,' in Michelle Perrot, ed., *Une histoire des femmes, est-elle possible?* (Marseille, 1984); Robert Nye, *Masculinity and Male Codes of Honor in France* (Berkeley, CA, 1992).

3 See R.W. Connell, *Gender and Power: Society, the Person and Sexual Politics* (Stanford, CA. 1987), pp. 18, 183.

4 See, among other works, Mrinalini Sinha, *Colonial Masculinity: The 'Manly Englishman' and the 'Effeminate Bengali' in the Late Nineteenth Century* (Manchester, 1995); Gail Bederman, *Manliness and Civilization: A Cultural History of Gender and Race in the United States, 1880–1917* (Chicago, 1996); Martin Crotty, *Making the Australian Male: Middle-Class Masculinity, 1870–1920* (Melbourne, 2001); John Tosh, *Manliness and Masculinities in Nineteenth-Century Britain: Essays on Gender, Family and Empire* (London, 2004); John Tosh, *A Man's Place: Masculinity and the Middle-Class Home in Victorian England* (New Haven, CT, 2007).

5 Louise Newman, 'Critical Theory and the History of Women: What's at Stake in Deconstructing Women's History,' *Journal of Women's History* 2:3 (Winter, 1991): 58–68, p. 61.

6 Joan W. Scott, 'The Evidence of Experience,' *Critical Inquiry* 17:4 (Summer 1991): 773–97, pp. 792, 793.

7 Denise Riley, *'Am I That Name?' Feminism and the Category of 'Women' in History* (London, 1988), pp. 1, 2, 3, 5.

8 See Michel Foucault, *Discipline and Punish: The Birth of the Prison* (trans. Alan Sheridan, New York, 1977); *The Birth of the Clinic: An Archaeology of Medical Perception* (trans. A.M. Sheridan Smith, New York, 1973); *The History of Sexuality, Volume I: An Introduction* (trans. Robert Hurley, New York, 1978); *Madness and Civilization: A History of Insanity in the Age of Reason* (trans. Richard Howard, New York, 1965). In this section, too, Phil Deloria has graciously offered up language we use in our book on how to do cultural studies, still in preparation.

9 Judith Butler, 'Gender Trouble, Feminist Theory, and Psychoanalytic Discourse,' in Linda Nicholson, ed., *Feminism/Postmodernism* (New York, 1990), pp. 333, 334; Judith Butler, *Gender Trouble: Feminism and the Subversion of Identity* (New York, 1990), p. 25.

10 Marilyn Lake, 'Women, Gender and History,' *Australian Feminist Studies* 7/8 (1988): 1–9, pp. 1, 6.

11 See June Purvis and Amanda Weatherill, 'Playing the Gender History Game: A Reply to Penelope J. Corfield,' *Rethinking History* 3:3 (1999): 333–8.

12 See Laura Lee Downs, 'If "Woman" is Just an Empty Category, then Why am I Afraid to Walk Alone at Night? Identity Politics Meets the Postmodern Subject,' *Comparative Studies in Society and History* 35 (1993); and Joan Hoff, 'Gender as a Postmodern Category of Paralysis,' *Women's History Review* 3 (1994): 149–68.

13 Joan Hoff, 'Gender as a Postmodern Category of Paralysis,' *Women's History Review* 3:2 (1994): 149–68, p. 151.

14 Ibid., pp. 153–4.

15 Ibid., p. 159.

16 Catherine Hall, 'Politics, Post-structuralism and Feminist History,' *Gender and History* 3:2 (Summer 1991): 204–10, p. 210.

17 Christine Stansell, 'A Response to Joan Scott,' *International Labor and Working-Class History* 31 (Spring 1987): 24–9, p. 26.

18 Quoted in Sue Morgan, 'Introduction,' in Sue Morgan, ed., *The Feminist History Reader* (London, 2006), p. 17.

19 Mary Poovey, *Uneven Developments: The Ideological Work of Gender in Mid-Victorian England* (Chicago, 1988), pp. 18, 19.

20 Morgan, 'Introduction,' p. 17.

21 Hall, 'Politics, Post-structuralism and Feminist History,' p. 209.

22 Morgan, 'Introduction,' pp. 14–15.

23 Mary Poovey, 'Feminism and Deconstruction,' *Feminist Studies* 14 (1988): 51–65, pp. 51, 52, 58, 59.

24 Jane Flax, *Thinking Fragments: Psychoanalysis, Feminism, and Postmodernism in the Contemporary West* (Berkeley, CA, 1990), p. 183.

25 See Louis Althusser, 'Ideology and Ideological State Apparatus,' in Louis Althusser, *Lenin and Philosophy and Other Essays* (New York, 2001; originally published 1971). In this section and that on Gramsci, I draw heavily upon unpublished work written with Phil Deloria, whose generosity in allowing me to use it makes these sections far more intelligible than they would otherwise be.

26 See David Forgacs, ed., *The Antonio Gramsci Reader: Selected Writings, 1916–1935* (New York, 2000; originally published 1988).

27 This is the example put forward by Trevor Purvis and Alan Hunt in 'Discourse, ideology, discourse, ideology, discourse, ideology . . . ,' *British Journal of Sociology* 44:3 (September 1993): 473–99, p. 497.

28 Review in *Hecate – A Women's Interdisciplinary Journal*, 3:1 (1977): 115, quoted in Martha Bruton Macintyre, 'Recent Australian Feminist Historiography,' *History Workshop Journal* 5 (1978): 98–110, p. 109. Marilyn Lake, 'Nationalist Historiography, Feminist Scholarship, and the Promise and Problems of New Transnational Histories: The Australian Case,' *Journal of Women's History* 19:1 (Spring 2007): 180–6, p. 185, n. 4.

29 Pat O'Shane, 'Is There Any Relevance in the Women's Movement for Aboriginal Women?' *Refractory Girl* 12 (1976): 31–4. Marilyn Lake, 'Nationalist Historiography, Feminist Scholarship, and the Promise and Problems of New Transnational Histories: The Australian Case,' *Journal of Women's History* 19 (1) (Spring 2007): 180–6. See, for example, Marilyn Lake, 'Colonised and Colonising: The White Australian Feminist Subject,' *Women's History Review* 2:3 (1993): 377–86.

30 See Aileen Moreton-Robinson, 'Troubling Business: Difference and Whiteness within Feminism,' *Australian Feminist Studies* 15:33 (2000), and *Talkin' Up to the White Woman: Indigenous Women and Feminism* (St. Lucia, 2000).

31 See Darlene Clark Hine, 'Black Women's History, White Women's History: The Juncture of Race and Class,' *Journal of Women's History* 4:2 (Fall, 1992), p. 126.

32 bell hooks, 'Postmodern Blackness,' in bell hooks, *Yearning: Race, Gender and Cultural Politics* (Boston, 1990): 23–31, quoted in Morgan, *The Feminist History Reader*, p. 194.

33 Frederick Cooper and Ann Stoler, *Tensions of Empire: Colonial Cultures in a Bourgeois World* (Berkeley, CA, 1997), pp. 3–4. See Nupur Chaudhuri and Margaret Strobel, *Western Women and Imperialism: Complicity and Resistance* (Bloomington, IN, 1992); Anne McClintock, *Imperial Leather: Race, Gender, and Sexuality in the Colonial Contest* (London, 1995); Antoinette Burton, *Burdens of History: British Feminists, Indian Women, and Imperial Culture, 1865–1915* (Chapel Hill, NC, 1994); Ann Stoler, *Race and the Education of Desire: Foucault's History of Sexuality and the Colonial Order of Things* (London, 1995); Claire Midgley, ed., *Gender and Imperialism* (Manchester, 1998); Susan Kingsley Kent, *Gender and Power in Britain, 1640–1990* (London, 1999); Ann Stoler, *Carnal Knowledge and Imperial Power: Race and the Intimate in Colonial Rule* (Berkeley, 2002); Philippa Levine, ed., *Gender and Empire* (Oxford, 2004); Angela Woolacott, *Gender and Empire* (New York, 2006); Richard Phillips, *Sex, Politics, and Empire: A Postcolonial Geography* (Manchester, 2006); Mrinalini Sinha, *Specters of Mother India: The Global Restructuring of an Empire* (London, 2006); Patricia Grimshaw and Andrew May, eds., *Missionaries, Indigenous Peoples and Cultural Exchange* (Brighton, 2010); Marc Matera, Misty L. Bastian, and Susan Kingsley Kent, *The Women's War of 1929: Gender and Violence in Colonial Nigeria* (Basingstoke, 2011).

▶ 5 Writing Gender History: War and Feminism in Britain, 1914–1930

1 Brian Harrison, Prudent Revolutionaries: *Portraits of British Feminists between the Wars* (New York, 1987), pp. 146, 144.

2 See Joan W. Scott, 'The Evidence of Experience,' *Critical Inquiry* 17 (1991), p. 787.

3 Millicent Garrett Fawcett, *What I Remember* (1925, reprint Westport, CT, 1976), p. 218. S. Bulan, 'The Untrained Nurse in National Emergency,' *The Englishwoman* 69 (September 1914), p. 267.

4 'Mothering Our Soldiers,' *Common Cause*, 18 September 1914, p. 438. 'Woman's Part in War Time: Care of the Home,' *Common Cause*, 20 November 1914, p. 551.

5 Committee on Alleged German Outrages, *Evidence and Documents Laid before the Committee on Alleged German Outrages* (Bryce Report appendix, 1915), pp. 14, 19, 107, 109, 111.

6 Samuel Hynes, *A War Imagined: The First World War and English Culture* (New York, 1991), p. 56.

7 Maurice Rickards and Michael Moody, eds., *The First World War: Ephemera, Mementoes, Documents* (London, 1975), item. 101. Quoted in Trevor Wilson, *The Myriad Faces of War: Britain and the Great War, 1914–18* (Cambridge, 1986), p. 706.

8 'A National Shame,' *Common Cause*, 28 August 1914, pp. 406–7. 'Notes and News,' *Common Cause*, 9 October 1914, p. 469; 'A Way for Girls to Help,' *Common Cause*, 23 October 1914, p. 494. Reported in *Common Cause*, 27 November 1914, p. 560.

9 See Paul Fussell, *The Great War and Modern Memory* (New York, 1975), pp. 334, 174.

10 Rebecca West, 'Hands That War: The Cordite Makers,' *Daily Chronicle*, 1916, quoted in Jane Marcus, ed., *The Young Rebecca* (New York, 1982), pp. 381–2. Mrs. Alec-Tweedie, *Women and Soldiers* (London, 1918), pp. 1–2, 26.

11 Quoted in Lucy Bland, 'In the Name of Protection: The Policing of Women in the First World War,' in Julia Brophy and Carol Smart, eds., *Women-in-Law: Explorations in Law, Family and Sexuality* (London, 1985), pp. 47, 32. Alec-Tweedie, *Women and Soldiers*, p. 85.

12 H.M. Swanwick, *I Have Been Young* (London, 1935), p. 252. D.H. Lawrence, 'Tickets, Please,' in *England, My England* (London, 1924), pp. 52, 62–3. H.G. Wells, *Mr. Britling Sees It Through* (New York, 1916), pp. 388, 386.

13 Emmeline Pankhurst, 'What is Our Duty?' *The Suffragette*, 23 April 1915, pp. 25–26. Mary Lowndes, 'The Recrudescence of Barbarism,' *The Englishwoman* 70 (October 1914), p. 27. C. Nina Boyle, 'We Present Our Bill,' *The Vote*, 19 February 1915, p. 504. C. Nina Boyle, 'The Male Peril,' *The Vote*, 27 August 1915, p. 727.

14 H. Tawney, 'Some Reflections of a Soldier,' *Nation* 20 (October 21, 1916), pp. 104–6; see Samuel Hynes, *A War Imagined: The First World War and English Culture* (New York, 1991), pp. 118, 117. Herbert Read, 'The Scene of War: The Happy Warrior,' in Peter Vansittart, *Voices from the Great War* (New York, 1981), p. 118. Ford Madox Ford, *Parade's End* (New York, 1979), p. 233.

15 Vera Brittain, May 12, 1915, *War Diary, 1913–1917: Chronicle of Youth* (London, 1981), p. 195; March 6, 1916, *War Diary*, p. 320. Vera Brittain, *Testament of Youth* (1933, reprint London, 1978), pp. 360, 217.

16 Mary Dexter, January 1918, *In the Soldiers' Service: War Experiences of Mary Dexter, 1914–1918* (Boston, 1918), p. 166.

17 Mary Borden, *The Forbidden Zone* (London, 1929), pp. 60, 155–6. Brittain, *Testament of Youth*, pp. 496–7.

18 Anonymous, *WAAC: The Woman's Story of the War* (London, 1930), p. 222. A F.A.N.Y. in France, *Nursing Adventures* (London, 1917), pp. 121, 116. Irene

Rathbone, *We That Were Young* (1932, reprint New York, 1989), pp. 219, 236, 394.

19 Cicely Hamilton, *Life Errant* (London, 1935), p. 117. Helen Zenna Smith, *Not So Quiet... Stepdaughters of War* (1930, reprint New York, 1989), p. 57. Borden, *The Forbidden Zone*, p. 60.

20 For work on the dismemberment of men in the Great War, see Joanna Burke, *Dismembering the Male: Men's Bodies, Britain, and the Great War* (Chicago, 1996); and Ana Carden-Coyne, *Reconstructing the Body: Classicism, Modernism, and the First World War* (New York, 2009).

21 Brittain, January 8, 1913, March 4, 1913, *War Diary*, pp. 26–7, 30–1. Rathbone, *We That Were Young*, pp. 139–40.

22 Brittain, *Testament of Youth*, pp. 165–6. Rathbone, *We That Were Young*, pp. 212–13.

23 Catherine Gasquoine Hartley, *Motherhood and the Relationships of the Sexes* (London, 1917), pp. 14–15, 18. Christabel Pankhurst, *Pressing Problems of the Closing Age* (London, 1924), p. 40.

24 Sigmund Freud, 'Reflections upon War and Death,' in Philip Rieff, ed., *Character and Culture* (New York, 1963; first published in *Imago*, 1915; Freud, *Character and Culture*, ed. Philip Rieff (New York, 1963), pp. 113, 114, 117, 119. Peter Gay, ed., in 'Introduction', Sigmund Freud, *Beyond the Pleasure Principle*, 1920: *The Freud Reader* (New York, 1989), p. 594.

25 Freud, *Beyond the Pleasure Principle*, pp. 613, 615, 621.

26 Sigmund Freud, *The Ego and the Id* (New York, 1960; originally published 1923), pp. 31, 34, 34–5.

27 Quoted in Peter Gay, *Freud: A Life for Our Time* (New York, 1988), pp. 451, 452–3. See also Eric J. Leed, *No Man's Land: Combat and Identity in World War I* (Cambridge, 1979), p. 6. Caroline Playne, *Society at War, 1914–16* (Boston, 1931), pp. 13, 16, 20, 28, 29. Magnus Hirschfeld, *The Sexual History of the World War* (New York, 1937), pp. 22, 32. H.C. Fischer and Dr. E.X. Dubois, *Sexual Life during the World War* (London, 1937), pp. 47, 48, 48–9. I am indebted to Chris Waters for directing me to this source.

28 Hirschfeld, *The Sexual History of the World War*, pp. 34–5.

29 Havelock Ellis, *Psychology of Sex* (London, William Heinemann, 1948; 12th impression), p. 124. Quoted in Jeffrey Weeks, *Sex, Politics and Society: The Regulation of Sexuality since 1800* (London, 1981), p. 149. Dora Russell, *Hypatia, or Woman and Knowledge* (London, 1925), pp. 41–2. See Jane Lewis, *The Politics of Motherhood: Child and Maternal Welfare in England, 1900–1939* (London, 1980), *passim*; Jeffrey Weeks, *Sex, Politics and Society: The Regulation of Sexuality since 1800* (London 1981, p. 127, 128.

30 Weeks, *Sex, Politics and Society*, pp. 200, 207.

31 Th. H. Van de Velde, *Sex Hostility in Marriage: Its Origin, Prevention and Treatment* (London, 1931; copyright, 1928), p. 9; Hirschfeld, *The Sexual History of the World War*, p. 17; Fischer and Dubois, *Sexual Life During the World War*, p. 179. Van de Velde, *Sex Hostility in Marriage*, pp. 13, 20, 22, 15–16, 17.

32 See Isabel Emslie Hutton, *The Sex Technique in Marriage* (New York, 1932); Helena Wright, *The Sex Factor in Marriage* (New York); Theodore H. Van de Velde, *Sexual Tensions in Marriage* (New York, 1931). Mary Stocks, *Still More Commonplace* (London, 1973), p. 20. Richard Soloway, *Birth Control and the Population Question in England, 1877–1930* (Chapel Hill, NC, 1982), pp. 211–12. Van de Velde, *Sex Hostility in Marriage*, p. vi.

33 F. W. Stella Browne, 'Sexual Variety and Variability among Women and their Bearing upon Reconstruction,' in Sheila Rowbotham, *A New World for Women: Stella Browne: Socialist Feminist* (London, 1977), p. 95. Elizabeth Robins, *Ancilla's Share: An Indictment of Sex Antagonism* (London, 1924), p. xxxix.

34 Quoted in Irene Clephane, *Toward Sex Freedom* (London, 1935), p. 204. Stella Browne, 'Sexual Variety and Variability among Women,' in Rowbotham, *A New World for Women*, p. 103. Rebecca West, 'Six Point Group Supplement Point No. 3: Equality for Men and Women Teachers'; 'Equal Pay for Men and Women Teachers,' *Time and Tide*, 9 February 1923, p. 142. Dora Russell, *Hypatia, or Woman and Knowledge* (London, 1925), pp. 1, 12, 24–5.

35 Russell, *Hypatia*, p. 37. Dora Russell, 'Marriage,' delivered at the Guildhouse, October 30, 1927. In *Guildhouse Monthly* 13:2 (February 1928): 53; Dora Russell, *The Right to Be Happy* (London, 1927), pp. 131–2.

36 See the theories outlined in chapter 1.

▶ Conclusion: Where We Go From Here

1 AHR Forum, 'Revisiting "Gender: A Useful Category of Historical Analysis,"' *American Historical Review* (December 2008): 1344–1429.

2 Joan W. Scott, 'Unanswered Questions,' AHR Forum, 'Revisiting "Gender: A Useful Category of Historical Analysis,"' *American Historical Review* (December 2008): 1344–1429, p. 1422.

3 Ibid, p. 1425.

4 See Misty Bastian, ' "Vultures of the Marketplace": Igbo and Other Southeastern Nigerian Women's Discourse about the *Ogu Umunwaanyi* (Women's War) of 1929,' in Jean Allman, Susan Geiger and Nakanyike Musisi, eds., *Women and African Colonial History* (Bloomington, 2001).

5 Austin J. Shelton, *The African Assertion* (New York, 1968), p. 159.

6 See, for instance, Catherine M. Cole, Takyiwaa Manuh, and Stephan Miescher, eds., *Africa After Gender?* (Bloomington, IN, 2007); Oyeronke Oyewumi, *The*

Invention of Women: Making an African Sense of Western Gender Discourses (Minneapolis, 1997).

7 More accurately, *baa elele*, or 'having usefulness.' Michael J. C. Echeruo, *Igbo–English Dictionary: A Comprehensive Dictionary of the Igbo Language, with an English–Igbo Index* (New Haven, CT, 1998), p. 268.

8 Victor C. Uchendu, *The Igbo of Southeast Nigeria* (New York, 1965), pp. 37, 34; Green, *Ibo Village Affairs*, p. 255.

9 Uchendu, *The Igbo of Southeast Nigeria*, pp. 15–16, 37.

10 Elechukwu Nnadibuagha Njaka, *Igbo Political Culture* (Evanston, IL, 1974), p. 59. For a somewhat different representation of the powers of wives, see Agbasiere, *Women in Igbo Life and Thought*; Nwando Achebe, *Farmers, Traders, Warriors, and Kings: Female Power and Authority in Northern Igboland, 1900–1960* (Portsmouth, NH, 2005).

11 Richard N. Henderson and Helen K. Henderson, *An Outline of Traditional Onitshia Ibo Socialization* (Ibadan, Nigeria, 1966), p. 11. Agbasiere tells us that there is a standard of 'propriety' manifested in women's food preparation work. See Agbasiere, *Women in Igbo Life and Thought*, 120–1.

12 Uchendu, *The Igbo of Southeast Nigeria*, p. 57.

13 Njaka, *Igbo Political Culture*, p. 38.

14 See Uchendu, *The Igbo of Southeast Nigeria*, p. 18.

15 See Stephan F. Miescher, Takyiwaa Manuh, and Catherine M. Cole, 'Introduction: When Was Gender?' in Miescher, et al., *Africa After Gender?* Bloomington, 2007; Oyeronke Oyewumi, 'Conceptualizing Gender: The Eurocentric Foundations of Feminist Concepts and the Challenge of African Epistemologies,' *Jenda: A Journal of Culture and African Women Studies* 2:1 (2002):n.p.; Oyeronke Oyewumi, ed., *African Gender Studies: A Reader* (New York, 2005).

Glossary

Agency   The belief that human beings are capable of understanding the world in which they live, and act in response to that understanding to direct the course of their lives.

***Annales* School**   A school of French historians associated with the *Annales* journal who emphasized the social and cultural history of non-elite peoples as opposed to the political or intellectual history of elites.

Berkshire Conference on the History of Women   First held in the United States in 1973 as an outlet for the sudden and huge outpouring of work on women, a triennial meeting of women's and gender historians drawing participants from throughout the world.

Castration theory   Formulated by Sigmund Freud, the means by which the individual represses those elements of bisexuality that he or she was born with and develops a gendered identity. It involves the fear of castration taken on by boys and girls when they realize that girls do not possess a penis, the belief that they have been 'castrated.'

Civil rights movement   The US movement of the 1950s, 1960s, and 1970s that sought to establish equality of political, legal, cultural, and economic rights for people of color, especially African Americans.

Deconstruction   Associated with Jacques Derrida, the process of reading texts to uncover the internal, hidden oppositions and contradictions that help to constitute meaning within the text.

Discourse   As used by Michel Foucault, technical speech used by 'experts' in the fields of the social and human sciences – physicians, scientists, prison administrators, educators, psychiatrists, and the like, incorporating the institutions inhabited by such experts and all the things that they did there. Discourses enable the exercise of power through the creation and mobilization of expert knowledge.

Empiricism Drawn from the Scientific Revolution, a method depending upon facts derived from observation and experiment to establish knowledge. It regards facts as always already existing entities waiting to be discovered, and relies upon belief in a one-to-one correspondence between knowledge and reality.

Enlightenment A European and American intellectual movement of the late seventeenth and eighteenth centuries which relied upon the methods of the Scientific Revolution and emphasized the use of reason to establish knowledge about human societies.

Existentialism The post-World War II philosophy associated with Simone de Beauvoir, Jean-Paul Sartre, and Albert Camus that emphasizes the importance of human existence and freedom. It posits individual actions taken in concrete human existence are what form the core of a human being, rather than any 'essence' that human beings possess.

Feminism The ideology that asserts women's equality with men. For varieties of feminism, *see Liberal feminism, Radical feminism, Socialist feminism.*

Gender Knowledge about sexual difference; the norms of masculinity and femininity fashioned for male- and female-sexed bodies.

Hegemony Associated with Antonio Gramsci, the exercise of power whereby dominant social groups persuade subordinate groups of the social and cultural rightness of the ideology by which the dominant group lives.

Ideology Systems of belief within which we move, often unconsciously, and through which we make sense of the world around us, usually without even thinking about them.

Interpellation Associated with Louis Althusser, the process by which the state 'hails' the individuals into their subjectivity.

Liberal feminism The belief that women are men's equals and that, by winning all the legal and political rights enjoyed by men, they will achieve equality in society.

Mentalité   Associated with the *Annales* School, the historical and anthropological study of cultural belief systems, especially but not exclusively among the non-elite populations of premodern Europe.

New social history   Arising in the period following World War II, this focused on recovering the histories of non-elite peoples through innovative methodologies drawn from demography, anthropology, and sociology, to name just a few. It posited itself in distinction to the traditional political and intellectual histories of 'great men.'

Object relations theory   Drawn from psychoanalysis, the body of thought that emphasizes the crucial importance of the child's relationship with its mother in its formation of identity, including gender and sexual identity.

Oedipal theory   In psychoanalysis, the body of thought that explains how boys and girls take on psychic feminine or masculine identity through their possession or lack thereof of a penis.

Patriarchy   Literally, 'rule of the father.' A concept used by women's and gender historians to explain the systems and means by which men dominate and exploit women.

Phallus   Associated with Jacques Lacan, the *symbol* of the dominance of men over women. For Lacan, the oedipal crisis took place when a child learned about the sexual meanings attached to various family members, accepted those meanings and rules, and took her or his place in the family system.

Postcolonialism   The analysis of societies and cultures colonized by European and American powers, often utilizing theories and methods offered by gender theory, postmodernism, and poststructuralism.

Postmodernism   A deep skepticism of the belief system by means of which westerners have ordered our thoughts and our practices since the time of the Scientific Revolution and the Enlightenment of the seventeenth and eighteenth centuries. Postmodernists contend that we human beings are always embedded in our surroundings, embedded by language, by history, by our social and economic relations. The knowledge we create cannot be set apart from conditions of life in which we create it: it is a product not of a pure discovery of what exists out there entirely independent of us, but of the kinds of questions we ask, which are themselves a reflection of the conditions of our lives.

Poststructuralism A form of linguistic and literary analysis based on the assertion that the meaning created in linguistic system is never fixed, but always
depends upon the historically particular discourse or text in which it is present.
It is the idea that meaning is fashioned not just by means of difference, but
by means of constant deferral as well, a continual slipping down a chain of
signifiers.

Psychoanalysis A branch of psychology first associated with Sigmund Freud,
the science of the human mind that posited that humans are not always rational
creatures but are often motivated to act on the basis of (usually unconscious) drives,
chief amongst which are desires for pleasure.

Radical feminism Radical feminists saw the root of their oppression in domination by men – in patriarchy and not simply in the economic or legal/political
system. They insisted that if women were to be liberated, they would have to
arrive at a 'consciousness' of their oppression. Some radical feminists became convinced that they would ultimately have to remove themselves from sexual and
social relationships with men.

Representation Associated with poststructuralist and postmodern thought, this
refers to the assertion that events, people, and objects do not exist out in the world
independent of our ability to articulate or represent them.

Second-wave feminism The women's liberation movement, arising in the
West in the late 1960s. Inspired in part by the civil rights movements in the
United States, and the new left movements in Europe, women in Britain, France,
Germany, Italy, and America began to demand freedom from the roles, portrayals,
and expectations that limited, diminished, and oppressed them.

Semiology/semiotics The linguistic practice of the analysis of signs – words,
images, gestures – which are made up of a signifier (that which is used to name)
and a signified (that being name).

Sexology The science of sex, undertaken in the nineteenth and twentieth
centuries by scientists, physicians, and psychologists.

Socialist feminism The conviction that the unjust class system produced by
capitalism and reproduced by the family rendered women unequal to men. The
achievement of feminist aims would follow upon its extinction. It is informed by
the insistence that women's work, experiences, and functions in a capitalist society
could not simply be subsumed into those of men within Marxist theory.

Structuralism   Structuralism derives from semiotic analysis, that is, the linguistic practice of the analysis of signs. It is based on the idea that words in a language are *arbitrary* and *relative*, that there is no innate connection between a word and the thing to which it refers; that is, that the meaning of words in a language is purely arbitrary.

Subjectivity   One's sense of self.

Women's culture   The trend in women's history to regard the private sphere of home and family as the site where positive bonds between women and a distinctly female culture were forged in the nineteenth and early twentieth centuries. This shared, female-only culture was seen to foster in women a sense of worth and a belief in themselves; it empowered them to venture out from their private sphere to engage in social and political reform activities in the public realm.

Further Reading

▶ **Chapter 1**

On the 'one-sex' and 'two-sex' models discussed in this chapter, see Thomas Laqueur, *Making Sex: Body and Gender from the Greeks to Freud* (Cambridge, MA, 1990). Londa Schiebinger's *Nature's Body: Gender in the Making of Modern Science* (Boston, 1995) demonstrates how racial, gendered, and sexual prejudices influenced the formation of eighteenth-century scientific discourses. Jeffrey Weeks's *Sexuality and Its Discontents: Meanings, Myths, and Modern Sexualities* (London, 1985) offers a clearly-written examination of how ideas about sexuality emerged in the modern period. In *Sexual Visions: Images of Gender in Science and Medicine between the Eighteenth and Twentieth Centuries* (Madison, WI, 1989), Ludmilla Jordanova demonstrates how the biomedical sciences informed western society's ideas about gender and sexuality. *Discourses of Sexuality from Aristotle to AIDS*, a collection edited by Domna Stanton (Ann Arbor, MI, 1992), provides an important set of articles about the construction of sexuality in the West from very early times to the present. See also Michel Foucault, *The History of Sexuality, Volume I: An Introduction* (New York, 1980); the collected works of Sigmund Freud, Jacques Lacan, Melanie Klein, and D.W. Winnicott. Denise Riley's *War in the Nursery: Theories of the Child and the Mother* (London, 1985), treats the theories put forward by Klein and Winnicott in an enlightening fashion.

▶ **Chapter 2**

As an eighteenth-century critique of contemporary ideas about women and gender, Mary Wollstonecraft's *A Vindication of the Rights of Woman* (1792 – there are a variety of paperback editions) is a powerful document. One of the strongest nineteenth-century critiques is to be found in John Stuart Mill's *The Subjection of Women* (1869 – also in a number of paperback editions), which he wrote with his wife, Harriet Taylor Mill. The second wave of feminist writers looked to Simone de Beauvoir's *The Second Sex*, which first appeared in 1949 and has remained in print ever since. Feminists such as Betty Friedan in *The Feminine Mystique* (New York, 1964); Shulamith Firestone in *The Dialectic of Sex: The Case for Feminist Revolution*

(New York, 1970); Dorothy Dinnerstein in *The Mermaid and the Minotaur: Sexual Arrangements and Human Malaise* (New York, 1976); and Nancy Chodorow in *The Reproduction of Mothering* (Berkeley, CA, 1978) took great exception to the theories put forward by psychoanalysts to describe and explain women's sexuality, and offered their own interpretations, helping to stimulate a great deal of feminist thinking in other arenas. One of the most persuasive critiques I have found derives from Jane Flax, *Thinking Fragments: Psychoanalysis, Feminism, and Postmodernism in the Contemporary West* (Berkeley, CA, 1990).

▶ Chapter 3

The literature produced by women's historians is vast, and cannot be adequately treated here. Readers may wish to take a look at the volumes of the *Journal of Women's History* and *Gender and History* for a sampling of the many articles that exist. For a series of overviews about the rise of women's history in the 1970s and 1980s, see Mary Spongberg, *Writing Women's History since the Renaissance* (Basingstoke, 2002). Bonnie G. Smith's *The Gender of History: Women, Men, and Historical Practice* (Cambridge, MA, 1998) examines the way gender informed how historians formulated the rules and regulations for the practice of professional history, defining the voluminous historical work done by women right out of the category. The work of Joan Kelly and of Natalie Davis on gender appears in *Women, History, and Theory: The Essays of Joan Kelly* (Chicago, 1984) and 'Women's History in Transition: The European Case,' *Feminist Studies* 3 (1976): 83–103, respectively. Joan Scott collected the essays that broke open the field of gender history in *Gender and the Politics of History* (New York, 1988). For an explanation of structuralism and poststructuralism, see Terry Eagleton, *Literary Theory, An Introduction* (2nd ed., Minneapolis, MN, 1998), and for Foucault's notions about power, see Michel Foucault, *Discipline and Punish* (London, 1977) and the *History of Sexuality, Volume I: An Introduction* (New York, 1980).

▶ Chapter 4

Many historical studies of masculinity exist that are well worth reading. In addition to the works cited in the footnotes to chapter 4, see the collection edited by J.A. Mangan and James Walvin, *Manliness and Morality: Middle-Class Masculinity in Britain and America, 1800–1940* (New York, 1987); the not-so-accessible Klaus Theweleit, *Male Fantasies* (Minneapolis, MN, 1987); Anna Clark's fine *The Struggle for the Breeches: Gender and the Making of the British Working Class* (Berkeley, CA, 1995); Paul Lerner, *Hysterical Men: War, Psychiatry, and the Politics of Trauma in Germany, 1890–1930* (Ithaca, NY, 2003). On identity and experience see especially

Denise Riley, *'Am I That Name?' Feminism and the Category of 'Women' in History* (Minneapolis, MN, 1988). This can sometimes be hard-going, but it is well worth the time put into it. Judith Butler's *Gender Trouble: Feminism and the Subversion of Identity* (New York, 1990) is sometimes hard to comprehend, but it is a classic work. Thoughtful critiques of Scott's gender theory include Gisela Bock, 'Challenging Dichotomies: Perspectives on Women's History,' in *Writing Women's History: International Perspectives*, ed. Karen Offen, Ruth Roach Pierson, and Jane Rendall (Bloomington, IN, 1991); Laura Lee Downs, *Writing Gender History* (London 2004); and Kathleen Canning, *Gender History in Practice: Historical Perspectives on Bodies, Class, and Citizenship* (Ithaca, 2006). For Foucault, see the readings for chapter 3, above. On poststructuralism, Chris Weedon's *Feminist Practice and Poststructuralist Theory* (Oxford, 1987) offers a reader-friendly account, as does anything written by Jane Flax. *Feminism/Postmodernism*, edited by Linda Nicholson (New York, 1990), contains a number of useful essays. Althusser's essays are collected in a volume entitled *Lenin and Philosophy and Other Essays* (New York, 2001), but are not easy to read. More accessible, Gramsci's writings are collected from a variety of unfinished pieces and notebook entries in *The Antonio Gramsci Reader*, edited by David Forgacs (New York, 1988).

▶ Chapter 5

The material from this chapter derives from my *Making Peace: The Reconstruction of Gender in Interwar Britain* (Princeton, 1993). Readers will find a broad literature on gender and war; it's difficult to know where to start. For just a smattering of what is out there, see Margaret Higonnet, Jane Jenson, Sonya Michel, and Margaret Weitz, eds., *Behind the Lines: Gender and the Two World Wars* (New Haven, CT, 1987); Vandana Joshi, *Gender and Power in the Third Reich* (Basingstoke, 2003); Victoria de Grazia, *How Fascism Ruled Women: Italy, 1922–1945* (Berkeley, 1992); Mary Louise Roberts, *Civilization Without Sexes: Reconstructing Gender in Postwar France, 1917–1927* (Chicago, 1994); Nicoletta Gullace, *The Blood of our Sons: Men, Women, and the Renegotiation of British Citizenship during the Great War* (New York, 2002); Susan Grayzel, *Women's Identities at War: Gender, Motherhood, and Politics in Britain and France during the First World War* (Chapel Hill, NC, 1999); Christopher Browning, *Ordinary Men: Reserve Police Battalion 101 and the Final Solution in Poland* (New York, 1993).

▶ Conclusion

For a treatment of how regimes of gender arising from different cultures can produce sometimes deadly confusion, see Marc Matera, Misty L. Bastian, and

Susan Kingsley Kent, *The Women's War of 1929: Gender and Violence in Colonial Nigeria* (Basingstoke, forthcoming). For other analyses of how non-western notions of gender play out politically in Africa, see also Ifi Amadiume, *Daughters of the Goddess, Daughters of Imperialism: African Women, Culture, Power and Democracy* (London, 2000); C.M. Cole, T. Manuh, and S.F. Miescher, eds., *Africa After Gender?* (Bloomington, 2007); Oyeronke Oyewumi, 'Conceptualizing Gender: The Eurocentric Foundations of Feminist Concepts and the Challenge of African Epistemologies,' *Jenda: A Journal of Culture and African Women Studies* 2:1 (2002); Oyeronke Oyewumi, ed., *African Gender Studies: A Reader* (New York, 2005).

Index